EIR (ISSN 0273-6314) *is published weekly*
(50 issues), by EIR News Service, Inc.,
P.O. Box 17390, Washington, D.C. 20041-0390.
(703) 777-9451

European Headquarters: E.I.R. GmbH, Postfach
Bahnstrasse 9a, D-65205, Wiesbaden, Germany
Tel: 49-611-73650
Homepage: http://www.eirna.com
e-mail: eirna@eirna.com
Director: Georg Neudecker

Montreal, Canada: 514-461-1557

Denmark: EIR - Danmark, Sankt Knuds Vej 11,
basement left, DK-1903 Frederiksberg, Denmark.
Tel.: +45 35 43 60 40, Fax: +45 35 43 87 57. e-mail:
eirdk@hotmail.com.

Mexico City: EIR, Sor Juana Inés de la Cruz 242-2
Col. Agricultura C.P. 11360
Delegación M. Hidalgo, México D.F.
Tel. (5525) 5318-2301
eirmexico@gmail.com

'We Are All Greeks'

—Percy Bysshe Shelley

EIR Contents

www.usu.edu

Note to Subscribers: *EIR* will not produce the issue which would come out on July 10. The next issue after July 3, will be dated July 17.

Free the Pope from Satan! Schellnhuber Is a Satanic Figure!

June 21—During the most recent days, John Schellnhuber, a Satanist in the service of the British Royal Family, has in effect declared himself Pope. Schellnhuber was fraudulently inducted overnight into the Pontifical Academy of Sciences, and tasked with explaining to the public the Pope's most recent, "green" encyclical—of which Schellnhuber himself was obviously effectively the author. This John Schellnhuber, who is a Commander of the Order of the British Empire, openly advocates, on behalf of Britain's Satanic Royal Family, that world population must be reduced to only one billion persons. He wants to kill off six out of every seven of us.

That the British Royal Family is purely Satanic, could not be doubted by any of the patriotic Americans who led us against it in the American Revolutionary War. Nor those who led us against Britain's puppets, the Confederate slave-whippers, in our Civil War. It was the British Royal Family which has time after time assassinated our best Presidents. The British Royals repeatedly, deliberately starved the Irish and the Indians to death,—most recently, when Royal puppet Winston Churchill starved at least three million Indians to death during World War II—all the while refusing American offers of food aid to India.

The Royals' eager propensity for mass murder has only increased during the reign of Elizabeth II, whose husband has repeatedly expressed the wish that he be reincarnated as a deadly virus in order to help solve the "population problem." And now Schellnhuber, the new would-be Pope, calls for the death of six billion human beings. A would-be Pope

The British Royal Family's Knight-Commander John Schellnhuber. Pope Francis capitulated to Schellnhuber on the encyclical Laudato Si'.

who is one thousand times worse than Hitler, no less.

In fact, the season of mass murder was already far advanced in the world, even before this atrocity in the Vatican. What else could we call the mass-drownings of refugees in the Mediterranean,—refugees from the "R2P" wars of Barack Obama, himself also a British stooge? Not only southeast Ukraine, not only the Middle East, but the United States is being stalked by mass murder as well. Now, the deep corruption now on display in the Christian Papacy, if it is not stopped immediately, likely means the early extinction of the human race itself. Don't just think of its effect on Christians. Don't limit yourself to remembering all the mass-slaughters which declared Christians have committed, supposedly in the name of their faith. The horror doesn't stop there. Think also of the Hell that this Satanic fraud is provoking already, now among non-Christians as well.

Yes, the atrocities of Satanists Hitler and Mussolini are like nothing when compared to the threat of British Monarchical control over the Papacy. If you wait to find out more, you will be dead yourself. Free the Pope from Satan!

Schellnhuber's Pedigree: Satanic British Empire Agent

June 22—Schiller Institute founder and chairwoman of the German patriotic BüSo party, Helga Zepp-La-Rouche, provided the following synopsis of Hans-Joachim Schellnhuber's pedigree as a personal agent of the British Royal Family, in her May 2011 call to the German people, "No to Global Gleichschaltung," which we expand here:

• After having founded the Potsdam Institute on Climate (PIK), Schellnhuber was brought to the United Kingdom in 2002, to assume the post of Research Director at the Tyndall Centre for Climate Change Research in Norwich, a branch of Oxford University's Tyndall Center. He was also brought on to the Oxford University Physics Department and the Environmental Change Institute.

• In early 2004, Queen Elizabeth II considered Professor Schellnhuber as the best man for a sensitive operation to pressure President George W. Bush into agreeing to the anthropogenic climate-change swindle. Schellnhuber traveled to Washington, D.C. along with Prime Minister Tony Blair's top science advisor, Sir David King, who is now the British Crown's Special Representative for Climate Change, appointed by the Foreign and Commonwealth Office in September 2013. The Bush White House reportedly complained to Blair about this mission.

• Also in 2004, the Queen traveled to Berlin to open the German-British Climate Conference, on which occasion she dubbed Professor Schellnhuber a Commander of the Order of the British Empire.

• In 2005, Blair turned to Schellnhuber to organize a conference on "Avoiding Dangerous Climate Change," at the G8 summit in Gleneagles, Scotland. The proceedings, edited by Schellnhuber, with an introduction by Tony Blair and IPCC head Rajendra Pachauri, were published by Cambridge University Press.

• With Professor Schellnhuber as chairman of the advisory board, the European Climate Foundation (ECF), from 2007 on, generously funded German "climate activists" from the above-named sources, while at the same time, Schellnhuber was working with the EU Commission on guidelines for the reduction of CO2 emissions.

• As German Chancellor Angela Merkel's current energy advisor, Shellnhuber bears the main responsibility for inducing Merkel to make the climate-change question the top agenda item during Germany's presidency of the EU in 2007—something which not only wrecked Germany as an industrial nation, but also seriously compromised Merkel's personal integrity as a scientist.

• In 2009, Schellnhuber, in close collaboration with Prince Charles, coordinated preparations for the UN Copenhagen Climate Conference (COP15). Preparations included another mission to Washington, this time to personally press the Obama administration on the urgency of the monarchy's global "decarbonization" intent, Obama's Science Advisor being fanatic depopulation champion John Holdren, a long-time associate and collaborator of Schellnhuber's. The Copenhagen conference nonetheless failed, after representatives of developing and emerging countries—and the Vatican—realized that the intention behind the climate question was massive population reduction.

• And in 2011, in his capacity as chairman of the German Advisory Council on Global Change (WBGU), Shellnhuber presented a master plan for a "World in Transition: A Social Contract for a Great Transformation," a proposal for establishing a worldwide eco-fascist order.

'We Are All Greeks'

by Dean Andromidas and Paul Gallagher

June 22—Stepping above the furious confrontation with banking powers over "Greek debt," Greek Prime Minister Alexis Tsipras observed on June 15: "I'm certain future historians will recognise that little Greece, with its little power, is today fighting a battle beyond its capacity, not just on its own behalf but on behalf of the people of Europe."

Touching the same idea two centuries ago, the great English poet Percy Shelley wrote lines quoted many times since, though never by the current German Chancellor, French President, or the IMF Managing Director.

"The apathy of the rulers of the civilized world," Shelley wrote in 1821, when Greece was a captive nation in revolt against the Ottoman Empire, "to the astonishing circumstances of the descendants of that nation to which they owe their civilization, is something perfectly inexplicable to a mere spectator of the shows of this mortal scene. *We are all Greeks.* Our laws, our literature, our religion, our arts have their root in Greece.

"The human form and the human mind attained a perfection in Greece," Shelley continued, "which has impressed its image on those faultless productions, whose very fragments are the despair of modern art, and has propagated impulses which cannot cease, through a thousand channels of manifest or imperceptible operation, to enoble and delight mankind...."

In the drama, *Hellas*, to which these lines were prologue, Shelley had a Greek chorus look on this scene:

Let there be light! said Liberty,
And like a sunrise from the sea
Athens arose!—Around her born,
Shone like the mountains in the morn
Glorious states;—and are they now
Ashes, wrecks, oblivion?

Today, for the sake of imposed debts, Greek cities and islands, in a mere five years' of dictated and savage "austerity," have been forced back toward the condition Shelley referred to, and Greeks back toward their living standards of a century ago.

creative commons/Steve Swayne

Civilization owes its very existence to the accomplishments of ancient Greece, wrote poet Percy Bysshe Shelley in 1821. Here, the Parthenon, which graces Athens' Acropolis.

But in the Greek government's attempt to break out of the "austerity trap," it is the wrecked economy of Europe as a whole which is at stake—standing before either a new financial collapse, or a revival in collaboration with the growth and the development institutions of the BRICS-allied nations.

Deadly Debt

The core of the fight over Greece and "its debt," is that the new Greek government, with a popular mandate, has been asking the European Union to shut down a tremendous Wall Street-London bank swindle and make economic growth possible again in Europe.

If that doesn't happen, the worsening bankruptcy of the whole trans-Atlantic banking system will continue to generate desperate confrontations with major powers Russia and China, with the threat of world war.

The rest of Europe, so far, has refused to shut down that Wall Street swindle, and on Feb. 18, Obama's Treasury Secretary Jack Lew backed up that refusal, including by a threatening phone call to the Greek finance minister.

The refusal to write down unpayable debt, by Europe's bankrupt giant banks and governments, is the fundamental reason the economies of the whole European Union have been dead in the water for seven years. Since the 2008 financial crash, these banks have sat with €2 trillion of toxic real estate debt on their books, tangled in tens of trillions in derivatives contracts—unable and unwilling to lend into the European economies, through year after year of economic recession and depression. Anything suggesting bank reorganization to deal with these dead debt securities under Glass-Steagall principles, has been refused, and Europe's bankrupt megabanks lie, like undead monsters, blocking the road to productive credit, investment, and recovery.

Now, the battle over whether Greece can adopt an economic recovery strategy has exposed the fact that large amounts of *government debt*, accumulated by various European governments bailing out their big banks, is also unpayable and must be written down—starting with that of Greece.

A Bankers' Coup Attempt

Speaking at the Paris Schiller Institute conference on June 14, Stélios Kouloglou, a European MP from the Greek Syriza party, exposed the plot by the IMF, European Central Bank (ECB) and European Commission—the so-called "European institutions" or Troika—to use the debt issue to overthrow the current Greek government.

Comparing the situation to the overthrow of Chile's President Salvador Allende in 1973, Kouloglou said, "Before Pinochet came in with the tanks in 1972, President Nixon told the CIA: Make the economy scream. And the banks cut off all credit to Chile."

Today, the coup is not by "tanks, but by the banks." As soon as Syriza came to power, explained Kouloglu, Mario Draghi of the ECB cut off, without the slightest justification, the main source of financing of Greek banks. He replaced it with the so-called Emergency Liquidity Assistance (ELA), a facility which must be renewed every week. This, he used as a sword of Damocles hanging over the head of the Greek government.

Kouloglou used the occasion to address bitter remarks to France: "Abandoned by those forces whose support it was counting on—the French government—Greece cannot solve the major problem of the country: an intolerable debt, which was used essentially to bail out French and German banks' assets in Greece."

The proposal for an international debt conference like that of 1953, which freed Germany from the greater part of debt reparations, opening the road to the economic miracle, has been drowned in a sea of threats and ultimatums, he charged. In that loaded climate, Russia's positive answer to Greece's request to participate in the new BRICS bank, came as a sigh of relief and optimism for Greek public opinion.

"We will resist,' Kouloglou concluded, underscoring that time is of the essence, best wishes for the Greek government are no longer enough, and the solidarity it deserves must be expressed by action.

Greece Under Siege

After returning from a high-pressure week of meeting in Athens, co-author Dean Andromidas can testify to the brutal evidence of the charges by Kouloglou of a bankers' plot to overthrow the fighting Greek government. The siege of Greece is everywhere to be seen, from beggars on the streets, to shuttered storefronts in Athens' main business district, and more. The blackmail of cutting off liquidity, something that would not be possible if Greece had its own currency, is destroying the Greek economy as much as the austerity itself. Banks are unable to extend credit lines to viable companies; even hotel operators are unable to get simple medium-term credit lines to refurbish their hotels. Large

Greek multinational companies have moved their headquarters to places like Luxembourg, because Greek-registered companies are unable to access credit inside or outside of the country. Such moves mean not only loss of jobs but tax revenue as well.

One Greek financial expert told *EIR*, "There is absolutely no liquidity. The economy is collapsing every day because of this." He added that small and medium businesses, one of the major sources of employment for Greece, are being hit the hardest; companies are closing down every day. Over three hundred thousand have closed. He added that no foreign investors can even consider investing in Greece because of the uncertainty being created by the siege being laid against the country.

The liquidity siege does not allow Greece to borrow short-term, up to three months, to cover temporary revenue shortfalls, making it impossible for the government to implement emergency measures to deal with the humanitarian catastrophe created by five years of the brutal regime under the jackboot of the Troika "enforcers."

Nowhere is the situation more dramatic than in the health sector, where the previous Quisling government reduced the budget by no less than 50 percent. The new Minister of Health, Panagiotis Kouroumplis, who is blind, and one of the most respected political figures in the country, has taken on the "mission impossible" of finding the resources to rebuild the system. Not only have the country's hospitals been stripped of doctors and essential medical personnel, but 40 percent of the population does not have health insurance, which means they are denied health care. The minister is attempting to create a community health care system to answer this need, which is a matter of life or death for thousands of Greeks who are now unable to access health care. The cutting-off of liquidity makes his mission virtually impossible: a recipe for more death and suffering.

Every aspect of the Troika's policy, which the government is trying to reverse, has been, and continues to be, genocidal in its intent. Greece's creditors demand cuts in pensions, which have already been cut by 25 to 40 percent. Hundreds of thousands of Greeks live on the reduced 400 Euro pension of their grandparents. In many cases we are talking about as many as eight or ten people relying on one pension. The creditors demand an end to early retirement. In reality, early retirement means government employees retiring in order to reduce the number of public workers. Ending early retirement means laying off workers and simply throwing them onto the street with no income.

The "creditors" are demanding even more taxes. In Greece the poor, the unemployed, children, and the unborn all pay taxes. The tax regime created by the Troika demands that the first euro earned is taxed, thus eliminating a minimum income not subject to tax, which has been the norm in every civilized society. All pensions are taxed, even the 400 euro pension that is supporting ten people. If you have children, you pay extra tax for each child, which is also unheard of in civilized countries. The divorce rate has dramatically increased since married couples pay more tax, thus in effect taxing the unborn.

Thousands of self-employed professionals, such as engineers, lawyers, and doctors, pay taxes whether they have worked or not. One IT engineer told this author that tens of thousands of engineers have fallen into tax debt, despite the fact that they have been unemployed and have no earned income; this leaves them open to the seizure of their homes and property because of tax debt. In 2014, 65 to 70 percent of the engineers did not earn any income, yet owe thousands in taxes.

The result is that thousands of Greece's professionals are forced to leave the country. Greece's main source of wealth is not its beautiful islands, but its well educated population. This is another case of genocide, since Greece has a relatively high number of engineers and medical doctors who could play a central role if the economy were expanding.

Resistance and the BRICS

The very fact that Syriza, which prior to the crisis would receive only three to four percent of the vote, and the Independent Greeks, a new party organized to oppose the memorandum, are now in power, is testament to the spirit of resistance that has taken hold among a large percentage of the population. Those of all ages have mobilized themselves. The young take to the streets and join the ruling parties, or are ready to re-elect the ruling parties if elections have to be held. One finds pensioned former government workers, including diplomats and economists, back in government doing the jobs of younger men because they are "fighting the fight of the lives," as one party leader told *EIR*.

Crucial to the success of this resistance is its ability to gain allies, and here the government has clearly chosen the BRICS option. In his speech before the St.

A mass demonstration in Athens against the imposition of murderous austerity by the international financiers. This one took place June 11, 2015.

Petersburg Economic Forum June 19, Prime Minister Tsipras made clear he was in Russia, and not in Brussels negotiating, because Greece wants to pursue a "multidimensional policy and engage with countries that are currently playing a key role in global economic developments." He explicitly mentioned the BRICs and the Eurasian Economic Union. He declared that "Greece seeks to be a bridge of cooperation" linking three continents. (See below)

Greece has already strengthened ties to China through its port of Piraeus, whose container terminal, under lease to China, has become the latter's main port of entry for its ship-bound exports to Central and Eastern Europe. Greece is linked to Russia not only through energy imports, but through sharing the same Orthodox Christian religion and a history of centuries of cultural and political interaction.

The June 18-20 St. Petersburg Economic Forum saw this cooperation between Greece and the BRICS go to a new level. On the sidelines of that event, Tsipras and Greek Productive Reconstruction, Environment and Energy Minister Panagiotis Lafazanis met with the directors of the new BRICS development bank; the latter stressed their strong interest in the cooperation between Greece and the New Development Bank.

Tsipras and Lafazanis also met with Gazprom's head Alexey Miller to discuss the extension into Greece of the Turkish Stream Gas pipeline. This was followed by a meeting between Lafazanis and the head of Russia's "Bank for Development and Foreign Economic Affairs (Vnesheconombank)," Vladimir Dimitriev, where it was decided to form a new company called "Energy Investments Public Enterprise SA." It will be owned by the Greek state, and with financing from Vnesheconombank, will build the Greek pipeline, to be named the "South European Pipeline."

Fraudulent, Unpayable Debt

On June 17, the Debt Truth Commission of the Greek Parliament issued a preliminary, but extremely important report on the more than 240 billion-euro debts which the "European institutions"—the European Financial Stability Fund, European Central Bank, and IMF—claim against Greece.

After extensive hearings and examination of evidence, the Commission found *all* of this claimed debt to be illegitimate, and that it should not be paid.

The findings strengthen the Greek government's position against these same institutions' demands for new, and suicidal, economic austerity measures against the

Greek population. Furthermore they confirm the analysis published by *EIR* on behalf of Editor-in-chief Lyndon LaRouche in late February of this year, which found that the so-called "bailout debt" of Greece was a huge swindle, transferring European taxpayers' funds, via Greek government accounts, to bankrupt megabanks in London and Europe.

The Debt Truth Commission's report says:

All the evidence we present in this report shows that Greece not only does not have the ability to pay this debt, but also should not pay this debt, first and foremost because the debt emerging from the Troika's arrangements is a direct infringement on the fundamental human rights of the residents of Greece. Hence, we came to the conclusion that Greece should not pay this debt because it is illegal, illegitimate, and odious.

It has also come to the understanding of the Committee that the unsustainability of the Greek public debt was evident from the outset to the international creditors, the Greek authorities, and the corporate media. Yet, the Greek authorities, together with some other governments in the EU, conspired against the restructuring of public debt in 2010 in order to protect financial institutions. The corporate media hid the truth from the public by depicting a situation in which the bailout was argued to benefit Greece, whilst spinning a narrative intended to portray the population as deserving punishment for their own wrongdoings.

Political forces in other superindebted countries in the Eurozone will also be affected by these findings.

LaRouche's February analysis had likewise found:

In the case of Greece, much of that debt was fraudulently piled on the country in the course of huge bank bailouts, in 2010 and 2012, totalling about EU245 billion. These rocketed the country's debt, as a ratio of its GDP, from 126% at the end of 2009 to 175% at the end of 2014. The impact on other national debts was equally dramatic: Ireland's, for example, rose from 25% of GDP before it bailed out London's banks headquartered in its territory in 2009, to 125% afterwards.

The debt piled on Greece in the past 12 years (since it joined the euro currency) is significantly illegitimate in regard to its causes and relationship to the real economy of the country. It cannot be paid in the next half-century, and it cannot be paid by continued cuts in employment, pensions, wages, health-care services, or by selling off national income and infrastructure.

'The Debt Should Be Cancelled'

The casino lending of the biggest London, Frankfurt, and Paris banks, the deliberate rule-breaking by the IMF and ECB regarding Greece, and the irrational intransigence of German and French officials have made Greece's debt both illegitimate and odious—a giant swindle.

The country went on a borrowing binge after joining the Eurozone in 2002, making its imports cheaper, and pricing its exports off the market. There are no irrational borrowers without irrational lenders, and the banks threw money wildly at Greece to finance German, French, and U.S. exports, especially military. When Greece reached clear insolvency by 2010, the banks refused to allow any debt writeoff. Instead, the "European institutions" started giving bailout loans with taxpayers' funds—committing the unbelievable "mistake" of lending new funds to a bankrupt which had no protection from its creditors (the London-centered banks).

The IMF and ECB compounded the mess by jumping in to buy up Greek debt from private financial institutions at 100% face value, violating their own charters and piling new, *shorter-term* debt on Greece. In 2012 the bank bailout process was repeated on an even larger scale, and 240 billion euros of new debt piled on, again with taxpayers' funds. Ninety percent of all 350 billion euros of the bailout loans passed through Greek federal accounts at the speed of light, and landed at the very same German, French, and British megabanks, allowing them not to write off their casino-wild Greek "debt assets."

On June 19, days after the June 13-14 Schiller Institute event in Paris and LaRouche's new statements, the influential senior former Social Democratic Chancellor of Germany, Helmut Schmidt, spoke to the Greek semi-official press agency, ANA-MPA.

While saying an "unorganized" Greek exit from the euro could lead to disaster, Schmidt said that Greece should never have joined the Eurozone, and that its problems could more easily be solved if it still had its national currency, the drachma.

YouTube

Greek Prime Minister Alexis Tsipras speaks at the St. Petersburg International Economic Forum on June 19, 2015.

When asked about a cancellation of Greek debt, as modeled on the London Debt Agreement of 1953 on German debt, Schmidt was clear: "I want to tell you that I think that it is completely excluded that Greece will be able to repay its debt. The majority of it should be cancelled."

Schmidt made his own proposal for a solution to the crisis, calling for a European investment program for the benefit of Greece, which can be financed not only from Germany, but also via an agreement to write off a large part of the accumulated debt of Greece. He also made clear that it is nonsense to say that the German people have been bled by Greece, which is what Germans read every day in their media.

A Way to the Future

LaRouche had called in February for full international backing for the Greek government's position, stating: "Looting does not constitute legitimate debt. The debt is illegal, it is unpayable, and it is the fruit of a London-led criminal enterprise that must be shut down altogether, if the world is to survive the coming months without an eruption of general war in the center of Europe. This [issue] has to be put loud and clear on every doorstep in the United States. If you want to avoid World War III, that's what you'll do."

He called for creating a "buffer of credit" for the real economy—a credit institution on Alexander Hamilton's principles. Such a new development bank in Greece will be linked to the European Investment Bank—and to China and the BRICS-allied nations.

One week ago on June 18, LaRouche said, "You cannot sustain the euro system, it is intrinsically bankrupt. If you base a 'debt deal' on that system—any 'debt deal,'—that deal will fail. The fraud of what Wall Street and London banks are calling 'their debt assets', has to be eliminated, because populations—not only the Greeks—are being beaten down by worthless claims. *Cancel* those claims. Relieve the nations of the claims of this speculation, these 'investments' in gambling bets, and an opening is created for internal economic development of European nations and the United States.

"The solution," he said, "is an international policy of Glass-Steagall banking; agreements among these nations to implement Glass-Steagall principles. Most important by far:" LaRouche said, "Restore the Glass-Steagall Act to force in the United States. That is the driver for this whole effort. That opens up the issuance of national credit for productivity and development."

LaRouche also addressed the campaign by forces behind German Finance Minister Wolfgang Schäuble, to force Greece out of the euro system. "If Greece goes out, goes back to the drachma, the negotiated value of the drachma can be increased significantly, and problems solved," he said. "It is not correct to say that the drachma must collapse in value against the euro. The pressure on Greece is coming from the London-Wall Street banking system, and the claims of that system are worthless. Its speculation on unpayable debt has to be cancelled.

"The euro will be falling because of its bankruptcy; the value of the drachma against the euro can be maintained, and may go up. Again, the critical action is Glass-Steagall in the United States, and force it in European countries. With that, the United States and Europe can generate national credit institutions, linked to the BRICS' new international development banks, and issue a surge of credit for productive employment.

"The Greek Parliament has thus done a service to the future, if we take the right actions now," LaRouche concluded.

'Why I Am Here, and Not In Brussels'

The Greek Prime Minister made this speech on June 19, to the St. Petersburg International Economic Forum in Russia:

I would like to thank the organizers for the great honor of inviting me to participate in this important event at the International Economic Forum in St. Petersburg.

Many of you may be wondering why I am here today and not in Brussels negotiating. However, I am here, exactly because I think that a country that wants to examine and explore possibilities for succeeding, must have a multidimensional policy and engage with countries that are currently playing a key role in global economic developments.

The economic circumstances that resulted from the global crisis eruption in 2008 have led to a very different world.

In Europe, we had long been under the illusion that we were the center of the world, taking into consideration only those developments occurring just beyond the borders of our neighborhood to the other side of the Atlantic.

The world's economic center of gravity, however, has shifted.

New emerging powers are playing an increasingly important role economically and geopolitically.

International relations are acquiring an increasingly multipolar nature. The role of the G20, the upgrading of the regional cooperation processes in Asia, Latin America, and Africa, as well as the strengthening of cooperation between the BRICS countries are irrefutable proof of the emerging new economic world.

Moreover, the Eurasian Union—this relatively new project for regional economic integration—is potentially another source of new wealth production and economic power.

Out of the Casino Economy

However, these changes do not, in and of themselves, lead to a more peaceful or a stable world.

The existing significant social challenges remain, including poverty, unemployment and social marginalization, while regional conflicts, crises, and tensions are intensifying. In the Middle East, Africa, the Black Sea region.

And in this sense, the great challenge of this new era is whether the shift in the global economic center of gravity will generate new possibilities for addressing these global social challenges and inequalities, or whether it will accelerate the uncontrolled course of the global economy—aptly described as a casino economy by the former President of the European Commission, Jacques Delors, shortly before the resounding economic collapse in 2008.

For the old financial center, particularly for Europe and the Western world, the challenge will be whether it chooses to react positively to new challenges by building bridges of cooperation with the emerging world, or whether it will remain committed to old doctrines, raising new walls of geopolitical conflicts.

The crisis in Ukraine, for example, opened a new wound of destabilization in the heart of Europe, a bad omen for international developments. Instead of greater economic and political cooperation in the region, there is a revival of an obsolete Cold War. Which leads to a vicious cycle of aggressive rhetoric,

The Kremlin
Greek Prime Minister Alexis Tsipras was in Russia June 19.

militarization and trade sanctions.

This vicious cycle must come to an end as quickly as possible; diplomatic initiatives, such as implementing the Minsk Agreement, are valuable and should be supported.

My country, Greece, is located in the geographical center of many of these crises and tensions; nevertheless, it maintains its role as a pole of stability and security in the region. As a European, Mediterranean, and Balkan country, as well as one belonging to the wider Black Sea neighborhood, Greece seeks to be a bridge of cooperation in its region. To become a hub of investment, trade, energy cooperation, transport, tourism, cultural, and educational exchanges at the crossroads of three continents.

We intend to capitalize on our participation in all international bodies that we are members of as a European country.

While fully respecting our commitments as such, we will also actively seek to become a bridge of cooperation both in our region and beyond, with our traditional friends such as Russia, but also with new global and regional organizations.

Eurozone Is the Problem

Of course, as you are all undoubtedly aware, we are currently in the middle of a storm. But we are a seafaring people, well-versed in weathering storms and unafraid of sailing in large seas, in new seas, in order to reach new and more secure ports.

Friends, the problem that we, and our partners in the EU are facing, hinges on the developments I have described. The EU, of which Greece is a member, must rediscover its true course by returning to its founding statutory principles and declarations: Solidarity, democracy, social justice. This will be impossible, though, if the EU persists with austerity policies and the disruption of social cohesion, which only serve to further the recession.

Let us not fool ourselves: the so-called Greek problem is not a Greek problem. It is a European problem. The problem is not Greece. The problem is the Eurozone, and its very structure.

And the question remains, whether the EU will allow room for growth, social cohesion, and prosperity. Whether it will allow room for political solidarity instead of policies imposing dead ends and failed projects.

Dear friends, the emerging new multipolar world will truly be innovative and pioneering if it can free

itself of the root problems fueling the global crisis. But this cannot occur—it has never occurred in history— without bold decisions. We cannot move forward in this new world while still carrying the burdens of our past mistakes. Otherwise, we will be doomed to repeat them and we will continue to fail—whereas the challenge for us is to change in order to succeed. To face new challenges and overcome them.

Thank you very much.

Whole Families Survive On Pensions of Elderly

In a June 19 "Letter to Germans On Pensions" published in the newspaper *Der Tagespiegel*, Alexis Tsipras injected some realities into the absurdity which lately has passed for discussion of Greek pensions in Germany—and at IMF headquarters. Here is an excerpt from the Greek Prime Minister's letter:

It may sound somewhat suspect that 75% of the primary expenditure [of the Greek government] is used to pay for salaries and pensions. If it sounds unbelievable—that's because it is: Only 30% of the primary expenditure concerns pensions....

The comparison with Germany's pensions is also rather misleading. According to the Aging Reports (2009, 2015), pension expenditure in Greece rose from 11.7% of GDP in 2007 (slightly higher than the 10.4% in Germany) and reached 16.2% in 2013 (while in Germany the numbers remained almost stable).

What caused this increase? Was it due to an increase in pensioners or an increase in pension amounts? The answer is: Neither. The number of pensioners has essentially remained unchanged and pensions have shrunk dramatically due to the implemented policies. Simple arithmetic is sufficient to reach the conclusion that the increase in pension expenditure as a percentage of GDP, is entirely due to a decline in GDP (denominator), and not to an increase in expenditure (the numerator). In other words, GDP declined faster than the pensions.

Concerning retirement ages, could it be that

in Greece, employees retire much younger? The truth is that the retirement age in Greece is 67 years for men and women, i.e. two years more than in Germany. The average exit age from the labor market for men in Greece is 64.4 years; i.e., eight months earlier than the 65.1 years in Germany; while Greek women retire at 64.5 years, about 3.5 months later than German women, who retire at 64.2 years.

I wanted to highlight the above again, not to deny the ailments of our social security system—but to prove that the problem is not one of supposed generous pensions. The most significant disruption to the pension funds is due to dramatically lower revenues in recent years. These were caused by the loss of assets due to the PSI (haircut of Greek bonds held by the Pension Funds, totalling approximately 25 billion euros) as well as—and most importantly—by the sharp drop in contributions that resulted from soaring unemployment, and the reduction in wages.

In particular, during the period 2010-2014, approximately 13 billion euros were removed from our social security system through a series of measures, with a corresponding reduction in pensions and allowances [by] about 50%, a fact which has exhausted any margin for further reductions without undermining the operational core of the system. Moreover, we must understand that the system is being mainly pressed on the revenue side and less so on expenditures, as is often implied.

I would also like to call attention to a matter that is unique to the Greek crisis. The social security system is the institutionalized mechanism of intergenerational solidarity, and its sustainability is a main concern for society as a whole. Traditionally, this solidarity has meant that young people, through their contributions, fund the pensions of their parents. But during the Greek crisis, we've witnessed this solidarity being reversed, as the parents' pensions fund the survival of their children. The pensions of the elderly are often the last refuge for entire families that have only one, or no member working, in a country with 25% unemployment in the general population, and 50% among young people.

Why Greeks Love Mikis Theodorakis—and His Music

by Theodore Andromidas and Dean Andromidas

Men like Mikis Theodorakis are rare. There is no more beloved figure for the Hellenic people. And he has come to represent, and still lead, the struggles of the Greek people against what have been centuries of war, against first the Ottoman, and then British Empire.

Born on the island of Chios in 1925, he spent his childhood in the towns and villages of the Greek countryside, becoming familiar with the music of Greece. It was in the Peloponnesian town of Tripolis, where he spent his teenage years, that he first heard Beethoven's Ninth Symphony, and decided then to become a composer.

Yet, you cannot really understand why he is so loved by the Greek people, without understanding his lifelong struggle, not just to defeat British-controlled fascism, but to create a new musical voice for Greece.

In 1972, when he was in exile during the Colonels' Junta that ruled Greece militarily at the time, he wrote this in the forward of the book *Mikis Theodorakis: Music and Social Change*, by George Giannaris:

Search as one may in the poetic texts that I have used, one will not find any political slogans. One will find neither obvious nor hidden propaganda concerning specific political viewpoints. Consequently, the politicization of my art is exclusively the result of two causes (a) its forthrightness, and (b) my personal commitment. This is the consequence and the cost that springs forth from my basic principle that art ought to communicate at every moment with the people. In other words, it ought to involve the masses.

The masses, however, are not something abstract but are, on the contrary, totally concrete. For instance, masses for me are the Greek people who today live under certain conditions that produce specific problems, expectations, ideologies, ideals. From its historical past, this people has inherited particular traditions principles, customs, sensitivity, learning and a specific intellectual and cultural foundation. Hence in order to converse with this people, at this moment, and in order to give it—with the form of an artistic work—aesthetic truths that will concern it, the artist himself, as well as this work, must be immersed in this historical reality. This means that he must be sincere, as his work, too, must be sincere.

This is the essence of the issue of the politicization of my work. There is, however, something else. Creative expression is, above all, an act of freedom. 'I create' means 'I am free; I become free.' The message of art is the message of freedom. Therefore, the art that wants to express, faithfully and sincerely, a people that struggles for its freedom, aspires to win not only the love of this people, but also the hatred of its enemies. It is a great, a consummate aspiration, which I do not hide; I have pursued it with all my heart.[1]

It was also in Tripolis that Theodorakis began this lifelong struggle against British operations designed to destroy Greece and its culture. The Second World War had begun and Tripolis was occupied by the Italians. It was here that Theodorakis participated in his first act of resistance against the fascist occupation of Greece, by participating in a massive protest on the 25th of March, the anniversary of the Greek struggle for independence from the Ottoman Empire. This was his first of many arrests; he was imprisoned and tortured, managing to escape and flee to Athens.

In Athens, Theodorakis began to study classical mu-

---

1. George Giannaris, *Mikis Theodorakis, Music and Social Change*, 1972, Praeger Publishers, Forward by Mikis Theodorakis.

Greek hero and composer Mikis Theodorakis, speaking against the EU memorandum in front of the University of Athens in June 2011.

sical composition, trying to create a modern Classical music uniquely Hellenic. His conception was not music for the workers to rouse them to action, but, in fact, the first effort to educate a Greek population that had never been exposed to Classical music. Therefore, he saw as his mission, the task of bringing the Greek people through a process where they could not only understand and appreciate great Classical music, but understand their own historical and cultural relationship to that music as well.

At the same time he joined the E.A.M., the largest of the resistance organizations to the German occupation. For the remainder of the war he took an active part in the resistance while continuing to study Classical composition.

First Symphony in Prison

In 1945 the Second World War came to an end, but the occupation of Greece did not. A British-controlled puppet government was immediately installed, backed by the British Army, and the Greek Civil War (1945-48) began. Tens of thousands of Greek resistance fighters were arrested and placed in British-run concentration camps.

But this did not deter Theodorakis from his political activities; he spent these years either in hiding or in prison camps, was arrested several times, and was severely tortured. Nonetheless, he struggled to continue his passion for musical composition. His first symphony was composed on the notorious prison island of Makronissos. It was also during these years that he became interested in Greek folk music.

With the end of the Greek Civil War, Theodorakis returned to his musical activity full time, but by 1963, the struggle for liberty in Greece began again. In 1963, Grigoris Lambrakis, a socialist deputy of the Greek parliament, was murdered under circumstances that left no doubt that high officials of the police, army and government were involved. Although Theodorakis had never taken an active role in party politics up to this

creative commons

Theodorakis in 1961, around the time he entered his active political career.

point, he was convinced to stand for election. Elected a deputy of the United Left Party in 1964, he was also made president of the Lambrakis Youth Movement (Lambrakides).

One thing Theodorakis has always understood is that Greek people tend to have very powerful historical memory, a memory that spans millennia—and, most certainly, more than the last century. This includes the liberation of Greece from the Ottoman Empire, a struggle which itself took almost of a century of struggle to complete. Then World War I began, followed almost immediately by the Greco-Turkish war that ended in catastrophe for Greece. This was followed by World War II, the British-orchestrated and bitter civil war, and a British-imposed seven-year military dictatorship spanning the 1960s and 1970s.

The undercurrent of these developments was the continued British imposition on Greece, of a generally hated Hanover Monarchy. The Hanovers are the same royal house of that genocidal maniac Prince Philip, Duke of Edinburgh, (whose father was Greek nobility) and were thrown out of the country after the fall of the Colonels' dictatorship.

'De Vulgari Eloquentia'

For Theodorakis, the Greek poets of the second half of the Nineteenth and first half of the Twentieth Century took on the same task, in terms of the Greek language, when they fought to write literature and poetry in vernacular, or demotic, Greek. At the time Greece was oppressed by a synthetic Greek called *Katharevousa*, created by academics after the Greek revolution as a "reformed" Greek, and used by the reactionary monarchy as yet another form of cultural oppression. These poets sought to take the vernacular instead, and educate it through poetry so that the language and the people could understand and express new and profound ideas.

Of course, Theodorakis knew this fight very well and began a study of its musical dimension, leading him to a study of traditional folk music. He discovered its roots in Byzantine music, but the lyrics of that music had become trivial and banal.

> The contemporary Greek folk song of the mid-century had one great defect: It was unbalanced. The more passionate and profound was the music, the more banal the text. My first efforts were directed, therefore, towards righting this imbalance. Poetry was without any doubt the most highly developed of Greek Arts; what, therefore could be simpler than the association of these two great achievements of Greek modernity: poetry and popular music?

Commenting on the effect this type of composition had on his Greek listeners, he said in an interview in 2004:

> Don't forget, for Greeks to listen and to sing the words of great poets in their everyday life, was and emphatically remains a serious/important step in the conquest by a whole nation, of high culture/art, purely neo-Hellenic in content, character and form.

And again, in another comment:

> People don't listen with their ears, they listen with their imagination. If they have one....[I]t looks as though at that time, the Greek *laos* (people) did have imagination, sensitivity, the

thirst for the new and a focus on historical memory.

The Ballad of Matthausen

Theodorakis' emphasis on composing songs, goes to the heart of his conception of the voice as the most important instrument, something he began to appreciate when, as a young man, he heard for the first time Beethoven's Ninth Symphony with its chorus.

It is at this time, after the civil war, that Theodorakis composed a unique series of song cycles, using modern Greek poetry: *Epitaphios, Archipelagos, Epiphania, Mikres Kykliades*, to name a few. What makes these works so unique is that they were all composed by poets who had fought against the pre-war British-installed Metaxas dictatorship, or in the resistance against the Nazi invasion, or the resistance to the post-War occupation. These include Yiannis Ritsos, who began his poetic career in demonstrations against the Metaxas dictatorship. And the Greek poet/diplomat, Giorgos Seferis, who was awarded the Nobel Prize "...for his eminent lyrical writing, inspired by a deep feeling for the Hellenic world of culture.'"[2]

But perhaps one of the most emblematic of his works at this time was *The Ballad of Mauthausen* cycle, in which he put to music a poetic cycle composed by Iakovos Kambanellis, a Greek poet, playwright, screenwriter, lyricist, novelist and survivor of the Mauthausen-Gusen concentration camp. Here is one of the performances of this cycle sung by Maria Farantouri.

Macrocosm and Microcosm

In 1964 Theodorakis presented to the Greek public his dream of a rapprochement between the two sides who had fought the civil war, in the form of an opera, *The Song of the Dead Brother*.

But by April of 1967, the British- and U.S.-backed military dictatorship took control of Greece. One of the first acts of the new regime was to place a ban on Theodorakis' work. Theodorakis went underground, issuing an appeal for opposition to the regime. Soon after, he was elected president of the first opposition organization (The Patriotic Front). In hiding, and later imprisoned and tortured once again, he continued to compose. International pressure for his release mounted, and he was allowed to leave for Paris in 1970.

In an interview just given to the German daily *Frankfurter Allgemeine Zeitung* June 23, Theodorakis was asked whether music can harmonize human and even political relations. He replied:

Music is a bridge. It voices the desire of man for society. Humans live in totally different, often far-away regions, countries, continents. The overwhelming majority of them will never become acquainted with each other, never talk with each other, know little about the other. But exactly these humans can all listen to the same music and love it. We have thousands of such bridges, music is only one of them. Unfortunately, there are also bridges that are not crossed. But through the times, a few outstanding personalities—philosophers, musicians, painters, writers—have always been kind of the universal currency of human culture and communication, with their voices.

And he had said:

I believe that Art was the only power that could create within us a microcosm in perfect parallel with the Cosmos. It could transfer the laws that define Universal Harmony, inside us. It could make each one of us miniature solar, and huge astral systems. So that each one of us can be tuned in accordance to the Space that surrounds us. So that our inner harmony can be attuned to the Global Harmony, and so that we can become living molecules of the one and only Harmony. This completion of ours, for me, corresponds with the supreme goal of life. Otherwise, we are just sweepings that move here and there in the winds of life until we turn into dust.[3]

---

2. Presentation speech by Anders Osterling, Permanent Secretary of the Swedish Academy.

3. Translation of speech "Universal Harmony, On the occasion of the international interdisciplinary symposium "Music and Universal Harmony" in honour of Mikis Theodorakis," 10 March 2006, Heraklion, Crete, 2006.

The Development of Manhattan's Alexander Hamilton Chorus

by Diane Sare

Because it's like a chorus, like a musical chorus. And what you have, is you're having a number of people who are learning how to play in concert. But this is not the musical thing as such, but it's the same thing as the musical thing: You're developing a principle of concept, and concert, and that's what you depend upon if you want to really build an organization.

Our commitment now is to development, professionally, with some people who are professional and some not, but who have an inclination for musical performance, and who can show that they have a potentiality of becoming successful, or being induced to become successful. And you've got to say that that musical idea, of a musical chorus, is as if you can imagine, all of Manhattan suddenly has become a musical chorus, resonating from the top to the bottom, and on the seas beyond.

—Lyndon LaRouche with the
LaRouche PACPolicy Committee
June 15, 2015

NEW YORK CITY, June 21—In October of last year, Lyndon LaRouche announced his intent to revive Alexander Hamilton's Manhattan to its proper national and international role as the center for restoring the unity of the United States of America. A crucial aspect of this, has been, and will be even more, the formation of a community chorus, based on the principle of harmony, as expressed above.

Today, after 15 years of insane Bush and Obama Presidencies, embedded in over a century of stupidity (see EIR Vol. 42 No. 24), the nation is not divided, but shattered. Americans have been driven to such despair and demoralization that many have become completely alienated from their fellow human beings. Where is the outrage in New York about the drought in California? Where is the respect from the young for the elderly? Where is the anguish of the parents over the future of their children? Communication between people is not even spoken, but is carried on by text, e-mail, Twitter, Facebook, Instagram, and the list goes on. Personal (as in, in-person) relations are largely relegated to the erotic or criminal.

On top of that, or perhaps as a result of that, we have a president who is about to plunge the world into thermonuclear war, while he indulges himself in fantasy-ridden snuff films about the killing of Osama bin Laden, or hosts orgiastic rock concerts, which are the moral equivalent.

That being said, there is a better side to the American people, and it emanates from Manhattan; explicitly from Alexander Hamilton and his collaborators' battle for the principle of the human mind vs. the bestial approach of the Virginia slaveholders: (see EIR Vol. 42 No. 19).

It is this human quality of the American population which can be most directly accessed though Classical music, specifically choral music.

A Choir is Born

In December 2014, a Staten Island grand jury decided not to indict a police officer who was captured on video suffocating an African-American man, Eric Garner, in an illegal chokehold. Demonstrations, marches, and skirmishes with police broke out all over New York City, in spite of the pleas of Garner's family for calm. The anger was already building because the Staten Island ruling came shortly after a November

EIRNS/Bob Wesser

The Sing-along of Handel's Messiah organized at a Manhattan church by the New York/New Jersey chapter of the Schiller Institute in December 2014.

ruling in Ferguson, Missouri not to indict an officer who had shot and killed an 18-year-old unarmed African-American man.

Members of the Schiller Institute in New York City decided, given the season, that it would be appropriate to hold a "Sing-Along" of Handel's *Messiah* dedicated to the principle that every human life is sacred. The passionate response of professional soloists, who donated their time to sing, and the gratitude of the audience of over 100 who showed up to participate on a few days' notice, indicated a desire in the population to overcome hatred and division with harmony and unity. The necessity of this endeavor was tragically underscored when organizers and musicians learned that, just in the very moments the chorus was opening the program with the canon *Dona nobis pacem* (give us peace), two young police officers had been shot and killed as they sat in their police car in Brooklyn.

Members of the audience urged the Schiller Institute to establish a community choir in Manhattan, and a few weeks later, the first rehearsal was held with a wildly diverse group of professionals, amateurs, and political supporters who had never sung outside of the shower. The group gathered in a rehearsal studio tucked away in a nondescript aging office building.

C=256Hz

The December sing-along, as all rehearsals and performances of the Schiller Institute, was held at the Verdi tuning of A=432Hz, and the choir always rehearses at this tuning, which allows the greatest resonance of the human singing voice, and transparency with the instrumental voices. (See "The True Scientific Musical Tuning" in this issue) It turned out that the accompanist for the *Messiah* sing-along, had been the accompanist for the legendary tenor Carlo Bergonzi, who had participated in a Schiller Institute-sponsored demonstration of the Verdi tuning 22 years ago in New York City!

The combination of the proper pitch, bel canto training, and musical direction from the Schiller Institute's John Sigerson have allowed this growing, but very young chorus to have a warmth and fullness of sound which surprised the professional musicians in the orchestra that accompanied the most recent performance of the Mozart Coronation Mass on June 6. One of the string players, who had just performed with another amateur chorus the previous day, commented:

I think I am beginning to understand this tuning question. Your chorus has a much more open sound than the one I played for last night.

The dialogue ensuing with these instrumental musicians has sparked their interest, not to mention the fact that they can play more freely when the chorus is not pinched and straining in an arbitrary tuning. As the chorus develops, so does the orchestra, apparently! Recruiting a "chorus" of instrumental players, i.e., an orchestra, is clearly a lawful part of this musical expansion into Manhattan.

Back to Hamilton and Greece

From Hamilton's time to the present, New York City has been the center, of not only trade and criminal financial dealings, as on Wall Street, but of scientific and cultural discourse, which is informed by the history of Hamilton's commitment to unify our nation. LaRouche estimates that up to 20-30% of this population is susceptible of being recruited to support this mission today.

It is in this spirit that LaRouche organizers have endeavored to build the chorus, which now has several new members each week. The members of the chorus range in age from 19 to 84, and the range in musical experience, as well as cultural origin, is just as wide. Professional musicians are joining for the love of music, and amateurs are joining because they "always wanted to sing." Somehow, it is becoming a more cohesive group every week, the more new people join.

What is the idea of chorus? What is its purpose? How does the human mind work? As in the Thursday night telephone dialogues with Mr. LaRouche, the participants become more familiar with their own minds as they hear the thoughts of others, and then they respond. As LaRouche described it:

My purpose is to get the idea of a concert, produce a concert of various people, and we're now

EIRNS/Bob Wesser

The Alexander Hamilton Community Choir's performance of Mozart's Coronation Mass, presented at the conclusion of the June 6 Schiller Institute event in Manhattan. Schiller Institute Music Director John Sigerson is conducting.

talking about 50, 60, or 70 right now who are hearing each other! And many of them are coming back; some are not there at certain times, but the overall process is that.

The function of chorus is twofold.

• One, it allows the participants to develop a concept of their own thinking, or singing, as it is a part of a whole. As in the musical chorus, the whole is invariably greater than the sum of its parts, as can be demonstrated with the community chorus; if you were to hear each voice alone, the variety would be, minimally, shocking, but as a chorus, there is a unity of effect.

• Two, the chorus has an effect on the rest of society, which is supposedly not participating in the chorus per se. This quality of chorus, as it relates to society as a whole, ennobles the population at large by lifting them out of the sense-perceptual world to a truthful domain which cannot be expressed in common language, except through metaphor.

This is the principle of the Greek chorus, which is understood by Shakespeare and used to powerful effect in his drama Henry V. Ironically, in the play "Chorus" is one person. Or is it? Who is chorus?

The True Scientific Musical Tuning

The following discussion took place on the New Paradigm for Mankind show of June 17 on LaRouche PAC TV.

Jason Ross: One of the main issues confronting us today is what the nature of the human species is. This is being seen in such situations as Greece where the Troika is trying to force Greece to make incredible cuts to its social welfare programs to the population, in order to pay debts which they simply can't pay. Greece has responded that of course they won't give in, and that the principle of democracy is at stake—that the government of Greece was elected based on the notion that they aren't going to give in to these demands. So how could the government do that? It would be violating the very principle of democracy on which European civilization is supposedly based.

Another aspect of this issue is the decarbonizing campaign that was promoted by the G7 in their idyllic meeting in the German mountains, where they put forward the goal of decarbonizing the world by 2100. How thoughtful of 10% of the world's population to say what 100% of the world will do over the coming decades. And this is also being pushed in the promotion of the Vatican's weighing-in on this, pushing on a decarbonization policy. This is not based on any science about actual climate change, global warming, anything of the sort.

The intent of these policies is to prevent human

EIRNS/Joanne McAndrews

The Schiller Institute Chorus, joined by singers and an orchestra largely comprised of musicians from the New England area, presented Mozart's Requiem (at C=256) in commemoration of President John Kennedy, on January 19, 2014.

development and to reduce the human species dramatically down to the level of a couple billion, as promoted exclusively by many of the top people involved in these campaigns, like Prince Philip or by Hans-Joachim Schellnhuber, who believes that the world is dramatically over-populated. And by not escaping from the kinds of concepts that look at things this way, by not getting out of geo-politics, we have a very real threat of thermonuclear war between the West (NATO) and Russia being created, because of Obama's presence in the Presidency. So I think that we definitely need another image of the human species, and I believe Megan has something to say about this.

Megan Beets: I am going to pick up on the discussion that occurred this past Monday between Mr. LaRouche and members of the LaRouche PAC Policy Committee, which was a discussion centered on the fact that, given that the trans-Atlantic system means doom for civilization, where is a future for civilization to come from? We obviously see the Win-Win policy being promoted by Xi Jinping, and being adopted by the BRICS nations, but the discussion on Monday centered around the principle which is really at the core of this: the necessity of bringing about within human society a coherence of mankind, uniting all the different expressions of mankind throughout the world around a commonality of principle and a commonality of a mission.

I am going to read a couple passages from that discussion to set the tone. LaRouche said:

You have to bring about something which we've lost in the United States. You have to build a certain kind of harmony, a human harmony where people of different talents become part of a common chorus, and the idea of the parts, the unity of the parts, the cooperation of the parts of the common chorus is the principle of a republican nation. And that's the way you want to organize people to organize society. What you have to do is to bring a consonance, a symphony of consonance together, of people where all are more or less converging on a common understanding of each other which is a correct one. So if you take Classical musical composition and performance, you have an ideal model for developing the minds of people. And the idea of the chorus is the unifying of a whole population to a common sense of reality and mission, whatever their other skills are, and they rejoice.

In another passage that I think is extremely relevant for what I'd like to go through today, he said,

The idea is having the true idea of harmony which resides in something which is a characteristic feature of the human mind. The human mind is prepared only to function with a concept of harmony. And the idea of harmony as harmony in the form of Classical song—choral work—is the model for all harmony in mankind and everything in life that's harmonious. The machine tool, everything around that you are playing with, is all a part of harmony, and if you don't have harmony, then you have disjunction and you have degeneration. It's that simple.

But the point is the principle by name is very simple; it's called Classical artistic composition. Music. Music is the medium for typifying Classical harmonic composition.

Now, obviously this concept of harmony—a harmony among peoples, a principle of unifying very different people, with very different roles in society, coming from very different cultural backgrounds, national backgrounds, the unification upon a common principle—is very different from the idea that dominates today in the United States in politics: popular opinion. Harmony is not railing on people to cohere or conform with a popular opinion, but instead to bring people to a higher discovery of a higher uniting principle, which is exactly what we are seeing in the process unfolding with the BRICS today. That principle of harmony, as we have been discussing it, is not only a musical principle. It is something much more universal which goes directly, at its roots, to the discoveries of Johannes Kepler.

Kepler's Harmonics

So our idea today of harmonics, modern harmonics as they are used in music but also in the way in which they are expressed by Mr. LaRouche, is rooted in the work of Johannes Kepler. Kepler discovered the Solar System, but in that discovery and through that discovery, he also established the modern form of well-tempered harmonics, as it's used in Classical music today, and as it was picked up on very directly by Johann Se-

FIGURE 1

Major Scale

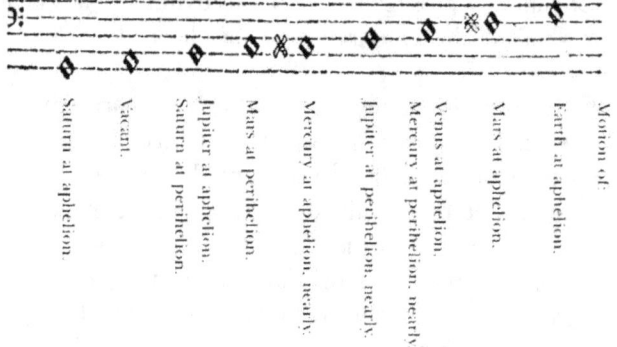

Minor Scale

Kepler's schematic of the planetary harmonies and their correspondence to the Classical music scale.

bastian Bach. I am not going to go through a full elaboration of Kepler's discovery here, but I will just say a few things to set up the idea.

Kepler dumped all previous assumptions about what the Solar System was, what astronomy itself was, and he discovered the Solar System as a physical system. The way that Kepler did that, in brief, is by conceiving of all of the motions of each of the planets and other bodies in the Solar System as an expression of the one mover—the Sun. Kepler imagined each of these planets as a member of an orchestra, playing a musical tone in a musical piece which is conducted by the Sun. A member of an orchestra is not an independently acting individual, which just happens to be in the same room as other independently acting members. You have a commonality of mission to play the same musical piece, and to play in harmony, to express the intention of the composer and also of the conductor who is conducting them.

You see here **Figure 1** that Kepler demonstrated that the fastest and slowest motions of each of the planets in the Solar System cohere to both a major scale and also a minor scale, as we have it in music today. As in music, the tuning of these scales, the tuning of these motions, isn't a one-by-one relationship with the Sun. What Kepler shows is that each of the planet's motions is modulated so that each is as harmonious with all of the others as possible.

And so what comes out is not a simple idea of tuning, but a much more complex, changeable, varied idea of tuning which we now see expressed in much more developed human music, string quartets, orchestras, and so forth. For Kepler there was no real separation between the physical process which he imagined, and then discovered in the Solar System, and the principles of human music which later came to be expressed in the most developed Classical music.

So this brings us to the real issue at heart with music. As you see with Mr. LaRouche's idea of harmony, and as you see with the way Kepler dealt with harmony, with music, you are not really dealing with sound. That might be a strange idea for a lot of our viewers. How is it that music isn't sound? When you go to a concert hall to hear a concert, aren't you hearing sound? When you rehearse a piece of music and you sing, aren't you producing sounds? Well sure, sound is involved; sound is a certain result that's involved in the process of performance, but music isn't actually sound. It's not built from sound. The combination of sounds does not make music. Here I want to read another short quote from Mr. LaRouche. This is from a few weeks ago in a discussion that he had with some of his associates. He said,

The music lies not in the music. It lies in the motive of the music. Otherwise, what does the music mean? It's just a form of noise making. You don't want to make noise. You want to capture the mind of people, not their ears. And the result should come through the mind, not through the ears. You interpret the thing not as it's heard—the heard sounds. What you should hear is the brilliant music of the unheard performance. You don't have to hear it because you are already captured by it. Your mind is an instrument. Your body and your soul are an instrument of music. It's not the music that makes that. It's the body and the soul which makes that. The music is incidental.

I think that that's a completely different idea of music than almost everybody—certainly in the United States and Europe—has today, and it flies in the face of what people accept and tolerate as popular notions of music: sound, entertainment, self-expression. What Mr. LaRouche is getting at in the short passage I read is that there is a substance to music which goes far beyond the notes—which goes to the capacity of the human mind to have new insights and discoveries about the nature of man itself, and to be able to convey and communicate these conceptions to other human beings. And that communication which we tend to call Classical music sometimes, can be clothed in sound, will be expressed in sound, but the motivation is this other passion of mankind.

Italian composer Giuseppe Verdi in 1886, when his fight for natural tuning was in full swing.

Now, To Tuning

With that notion of music, which is the notion of music of the Classical tradition that Western Civilization was founded upon—as an aside, it also resonates very strongly with the notions of music and art that you find expressed by people like Confucius—with that standard of art, what I would like to do now is take up a discussion of a very important specific "issue," you could say, in how art is performed today, and in the possibility of continuing the performance and composition of Classical music into the future. That issue is the notion of tuning.

It is a fact today that almost every single Classical musician—we'll leave the other ones aside—on the planet today, be they professional or amateur, sings or plays out of tune. Out of tune in the sense that they are singing at the wrong pitch.

What is meant by that: singing at the wrong pitch? Well, today as always when you go to a concert hall and you sit down and the orchestra begins to play—before you got there, or before the performance started, the musicians tuned their instruments. There was a standard pitch which was played which all the musicians tuned their instruments to. This would also happen if you went to a concert where there is a piano on the stage and you have a piano concert, or a singing concert with a piano accompanying. There is a standard pitch which was chosen, and all the notes were tuned to conform to that pitch as standard.

In most cases today, the standard pitch which is chosen to determine the tuning pitch of all the instruments, and which determines the pitch at which the singers sing their songs, in most cases is high, arbitrarily higher than it should be. In some cases it is much, much higher than it should be, meaning that every note that's sounded is actually a little bit or a lot higher than is natural.

Now this may sound like an issue for music specialists or concert aficionados, but this is not an academic issue; this is not an issue which is a debate within the "music world," and which has no consequence for politics or anything else. This is an intensely political fight. This is a political fight which was waged more than a hundred years ago by Giuseppe Verdi, the great opera composer, who was also a senator in the first parliament of Italy. This is also a political fight which was begun by Lyndon LaRouche in the 1980s and continues up to today. I will come back to some of the details of that.

But why is this a political fight? And why can you say that there is such a thing as a right or a wrong pitch? How can you say that an orchestra is tuned wrong? Who has the authority to say that?

Well, nature. Nature has the authority to say that. The human voice has the authority to say what pitch it wants to sing at—how it works best. All music today, be it vocal music, instrumental music, piano music, whatever, all music inherently is based on the human voice and the characteristics of expression of music based in human poetry and the human voice, and specifically, the trained human voice, as trained by discovered principles of how the human voice actually works, developed from the Renaissance on.

The human voice operates best when it's tuned to a particular pitch. It does not operate well when it's stretched to sing at a higher pitch or even a much lower pitch. The pitch which was agreed upon by the best Classical musicians of the Nineteenth Century and some beyond in the Twentieth Century is a pitch where middle C—people who don't know what middle C is could imagine a piano keyboard, and the note C right at the center of the keyboard is "middle C"—is tuned to 256 vibrations per second. So the correct pitch of that note, or the string of the piano of that note, is 256 Hz, 256 vibrations per second. If it were more, the note would sound a little bit higher in pitch to you, and if it were less, it would sound a little bit lower. So the proper natural pitch is C at 256, which corresponds to the note above it of A at around 432.

I know that to people who don't play an instrument or sing, that may sound kind of arbitrary, so let me play a few examples for you. The first example you will hear is the tone A at the natural tuning of 432. Now I'll play the same note, A, at the tuning which is adopted in many orchestras in the United States, A440. You can hear that it is a little bit higher in pitch. It's a small difference, but it's a difference, and every note of the scale is adjusted up at least that much.

Now let me play one more tuning of the note A, A450, which is adopted in many orchestras around the world today.

Ross: That's a pretty big difference.

Beets: That's a very big difference—it's almost a half step, the difference between two keys on a piano, two entirely different notes.

Now, what's the result of doing this? First, I'll talk about the voices. What's the result of a trained opera singer who shows up in Vienna, for example? The Vienna Philharmonic Orchestra adopts a tuning today which is close to the highest A that I just played. An opera singer who shows up in Vienna to sing an opera role, where the tuning is much higher than the natural tuning, what's the result?

Well, back in the 1980s and '90s when the Schiller Institute was running an intensive campaign to return the tuning to low tuning, we approached many, many of the top opera singers in the world on this issue, and all of them agreed: The high tuning damages the voices. It stretches the voices. It makes the voices shift and change (in the way that they have to with the proper training) in the wrong place, and puts a strain on them.

It shortens the careers of singers, and also makes some of the music which was composed in the past at lower tunings unsingable. It actually makes it, in a sense, unavailable to modern audiences because you don't have the voices around to sing that music anymore, because of the strain of these arbitrarily high tunings.

Another result is not just on voices—again this isn't just an issue of the human voice, while instrumental music can do whatever it wants. You also have an incredible damage to the musical instruments—violins for example. For a violin which was built to play at the lower tuning of A432, if we tighten all the strings to meet the higher tuning, there is now more than 8 pounds of additional pressure on the body of the violin than there is at the lower tuning. Over time this causes tremendous damage to this great wealth of Stradivarius violins, and all of the other wonderful instruments that have become part of human society, human culture.

Therefore, I think the obvious question, given that the tuning varies so much from place to place (you never know what you're going to get from one concert hall to the next), and that the higher tunings do so much damage to voices and instruments: who would want to do that? Why would you want to do something unnatural? How did it get to be that way? Did people just forget what the natural tuning was and start to choose whatever they wanted?

No, that didn't happen. The real fight around the nature of tuning is a fight over the nature of man, and it's a fight over what music is. What is the purpose of music in society? What is the nature of the mind and the life of mankind? That's what's at the root of the fight around tuning.

Verdi Launches the Fight

Let me briefly give a sketch of some of the history of the fight over tuning pitch. As I mentioned before, and as I'll mention again when we get to it in the timeline, Verdi fought for legislation on this question in the 1880s, and LaRouche launched a campaign in 1986 to legislate the standardization of international tuning pitch at the low natural tuning of C256 or A432. But the fight goes back much earlier.

First, let's start with the Classical composers—Bach, Mozart, Haydn, Händel. In their time, there really wasn't a standardized pitch. You could travel from city to city, church to church, which usually would have an organ, and the tuning would vary widely. However, what is known is that the tuning generally used by these composers was much, much lower than the modern pitches. For example, both Händel and Mozart used a pitch which was even a little bit lower than the A432 that I played for you. Verdi asked for exactly this pitch of A432 as the natural scientific pitch.

The first attempt, which was a certain unofficial attempt to standardize the tuning pitch came with the 1815 Congress of Vienna. The Congress of Vienna was the international conference held at the end of the Napoleonic wars to set up a new political structure of Europe. What really happened at the Congress of Vienna was the re-imposition of fascism over Europe by the imperial powers. At the Congress of Vienna the Czar of Russia gifted a set of musical instruments to the Austrian Military Band which were all at the new high tuning of A440.

This wasn't just a whim on the part of the Czar of Russia; there was a political operation coming out of the Congress of Vienna to begin imposing a new, higher pitch in music throughout Europe. The new band instruments had a much brighter sound, a much more dazzling sound, and there are physical acoustical reasons for that which I won't get into today, but they had a sound which had much more physical impact on the listener. This set off a total craze, which I am sure was also created, not just a natural craze. There was a cultural operation begun from this time, where orchestras and bands across Europe began to raise the tuning of their instruments.

For example, the London Philharmonic in 1820 tuned to A432. In 1842 they had gone up to A440 and by 1850 they were at A452. Something similar happened with the Paris orchestra, and many other orchestras. While you still had people playing at the lower tuning, generally the pitches began to rise all across Europe, such that by 1877 at the Wagner Festival in London, they were playing at A455, which is much more than a half step higher than the natural tuning. In New York City in 1880 the Steinway factory was tuning their pianos to A457, which is extremely high.

In 1858 there was a conference held in Paris, which was largely due to the efforts of the composer Gioachino Rossini, who composed for the bel canto human voice, to standardize the pitch.

The idea was: this higher pitch is insane, we are losing our music, we are losing our voices, we have to standardize the pitch! And the conference in Paris officially adopted a standard of A435, which is very close to the low natural tuning, and which was the lowest

A lithograph of Italian composer Gioachino Rossini by F. Perrin, done around 1850.

pitch in use in France in those days. In 1881, in Italy, there was a Congress of Italian Musicians, largely inspired by what occurred in Paris, which officially called for Italy to adopt a similar standard in tuning of A432. Now this was supported, as I mentioned, by the composer Verdi. After the resolution of the Congress of Italian Musicians, Verdi wrote a letter to the Italian government which reads as follows:

Since France has adopted a standard pitch, I advise that the example should also be followed by us, and I formally request that the orchestras of various cities of Italy among them that of La Scala and Milan to lower the tuning fork to conform to the standard French one. If the musical commission instituted by our government believes for mathematical exigencies that we should reduce the 435 to 432, the difference is so small that I associate myself with it willingly. It would be an extremely grave error to adopt as proposed by Rome a standard pitch of A450. I also am of the opinion with you that the lowering of the tuning in no way takes away the sonority or the liveliness of the execution, but it gives on the contrary something more noble of a greater fullness and majesty than the shrieks of a too high tuning fork could give. For my part I would like a single tuning to be adopted in the whole musical world. The musical language is universal. Why then would the note which has the name A in Paris or Milan have to become a B flat in Rome?

In 1884, three years later, the Italian government did officially adopt A432 as the standard tuning pitch for all orchestras of Italy. Similar motions were taken up in other countries, Spain, for example, Belgium. In 1885 there was an international conference in Vienna which turned out to be a huge fight. Verdi sent his friend Boito, who was his librettist and who he worked with very closely. Verdi instructed Boito to fight like hell for 432, or 435 if he had to. While that conference was a little

Hitler's Minister of Propaganda Josef Goebbels.

bit conflicted, and they did eventually resolve for 435, the point is that this was a political fight—and it never quite took hold, and Verdi recognized this. He actually banned performances of his opera *Otello* if they were going to be at the high tuning.

The Fascists Pull a Coup

Now I am going to fast forward a little bit, to 1939 when you had the next major attempt to standardize the pitch internationally. This attempt was led straight from Berlin by the Minister of Propaganda, Joseph Goebbels. So from Nazi Germany comes the request to London to please set up a conference to standardize the international tuning pitch at the same pitch that was used by Radio Berlin: A440, the higher tuning. This conference did demand a standardization at A440 at the request of the Third Reich, but obviously there was a lot of tumult and chaos in the world at that time, so this pitch wasn't actually adopted everywhere as requested.

I want to mention something else, at this point, for people to think about. We've gone through a sweep from 1815, really from the period of Bach and Mozart through 1815, and then through the time of Verdi, and now up to World War II. What's been happening to

music throughout this time?

There has been a great attack on Classical music, especially after Brahms died in 1897, and you have the promotion of an idea of music which is completely based in the senses, the sensuous effect of music. This came with Richard Wagner, the promotion of Wagner, the promotion of Richard Strauss, the promotion of Igor Stravinsky, whose best known work is *The Rite of Spring*, which is a musical portrayal of human sacrifice, all to create physiological sense effects in the human being, and to promote the idea that ugliness is music. That is what has been happening to music over the course of this parallel rise in the tuning, and this is obviously completely contrary to the idea of music as expressed in the quote I read from Mr. LaRouche about the powers of the human mind, of discovery.

There are more attempts made after World War II to standardize the pitch, which, for the most part, begin to take hold. Even in the 1930s and '40s, while the pitches were rising in concert halls, it was still agreed upon that the scientific pitch was C256. Here are two examples **Figure 2**. One is actually a physics manual released by the U.S. Army, which says right away that the scientific pitch is C at 256. The other example is from a phonetics textbook from 1931, which again asserts that C256 is the scientific tuning, and that if you raise the tuning, sopranos and others have a hard time singing music. Yet, the pitch has risen throughout this period. As I mentioned a few minutes ago, in Vienna the standard pitch is A444, and in Berlin it is A448, which is incredibly high.

LaRouche's Fight for Classical Tuning

Now I'd like to get to what the LaRouche organization has done since 1986 to fight for restoration of the lower natural tuning, to save Classical music and to save this precious power within society. In 1986, as I mentioned, LaRouche launches the campaign to save Classical music, calling for legislation to lower the

FIGURE 2

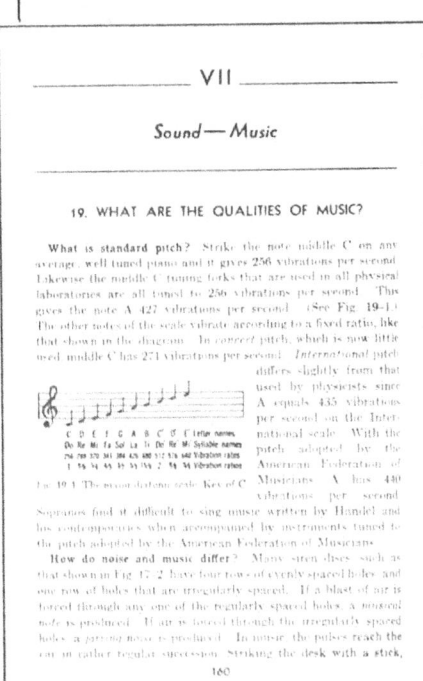

tute in the middle. Next to her is the great baritone, Piero Cappuccilli, accompanied by others including the Senators from Italy. This is Carlo Bergonzi, who gave a seminar with the Schiller Institute at Carnegie Hall in New York City demonstrating the superiority of the lower tuning.

Now I'd like to show a clip of one of the demonstrations that was done. This was in 1988 in Milan, which was the first of such seminars. You'll hear Piero Cappuccilli. Other people who spoke there were Helga Zepp-LaRouche, the chairwoman of the Schiller Institute, and Renata Tebaldi, who's one of the greatest operatic sopranos. Interestingly Tebaldi made the point that the high tuning doesn't just affect sopranos or tenors, or people who have to sing high notes; it's not about that. It's about the natural placement of the voice. She said that even basses, altos, and mezzo-sopranos who have to sing low notes are adversely affected by this displacement of the human voice.

What you will hear in the video is a short passage from an opera aria by Verdi. You'll hear it three times: once at the low tuning, then at the high tuning, and then once more at the low tuning again. Something Cappuc-

tuning. By 1988 we had contacted the top singers in the world. A couple hundred of them had signed our petition supporting such a call and we worked with two Senators in the Italian Parliament to introduce legislation in Italy, once again, to lower the tuning pitch.

Our organization sponsored seminars with demonstrations of the low tuning versus the high tuning, and the more truthful expression of the music which is heard at the lower tuning, as opposed to the higher. We eventually got thousands of signers to this petition, including Placido Domingo; Carlo Bergonzi, a famous tenor; Piero Cappuccilli, Mirella Freni, and many, many others. Additional signers were singing teachers, instrumental musicians, all calling for this. Here are a few pictures from this campaign.

This is a press conference announcing the legislation. Here you see Liliana Gorini, who is the Italian representative of the Schiller Insti-

Schiller Institute

The July 1988 press conference announcing introduction of legislation mandating the lower tuning in the Italian Senate. Schiller Institute leader Liliana Gorini (center) is joined by Baritone Piero Cappuccilli (on her left) and the Senators (Carl Boggio and Pietro Mezzapesa) who introduced the bill.

Schiller Institute

Tenor Carlo Bergonzi at his 1993 Master Class demonstrating the Verdi pitch, held at Carnegie Hall in New York City.

cilli points out during the demonstration is that when the tuning was artificially high, he had to do things to shift his voice on the highest notes which Verdi didn't intend. He said it changes the color....

Liona Fan-Chiang: He didn't intend to make color change at that point.

Beets: Exactly, but the voice had to, in a certain strained kind of way.

The campaign which this demonstration was a part of, unleashed a total brawl, a total freak-out, and the legislation that was introduced in 1988 was eventually defeated as a result of intense pressure from the United States on the Italian government not to pass it. It should make people think: if music is just whatever you like, why would something like this be such an issue? Why would the oligarchy go to such efforts back in 1815, and obviously recently, in 1988, to stop an effort to standardize the tuning pitch?

What's really the issue here? The issue comes back to: what is man? What is the power of music for mankind? Is it arbitrary? Is it whatever you want? What does

that lead to? Look around society today. Look at the entertainment culture that that has led to the situation of today, versus what would be possible if we had a culture which was dedicated to the truthfulness of this kind of music, of the kind of principles that are involved in developing and maintaining that kind of music in society.

I think that that is absolutely the core of our political mission today, and it is something which the United States and Europe, in particular, can give as our offering of some of the best of our culture to this collaborative process taking shape in the world today.

Fan-Chiang: It's almost as if you disallowed the universalization of language—as though you were to say: "No, you can't have a national language. It should be arbitrary, however you would like to, whatever types of noises you would like to make, that should be your way of communication."

Ross: All the gesturing that Cappuccilli was making in the video, I'm glad you pointed out what he was referring to—that he was changing the color of his voice to sing notes in different ways. As you had mentioned

Schiller Institute

Baritone Piero Cappuccilli demonstrates the Verdi pitch at the Schiller Institute's first conference on scientific tuning at the Casa Verdi in Milan in April 1988.

FIGURE 2

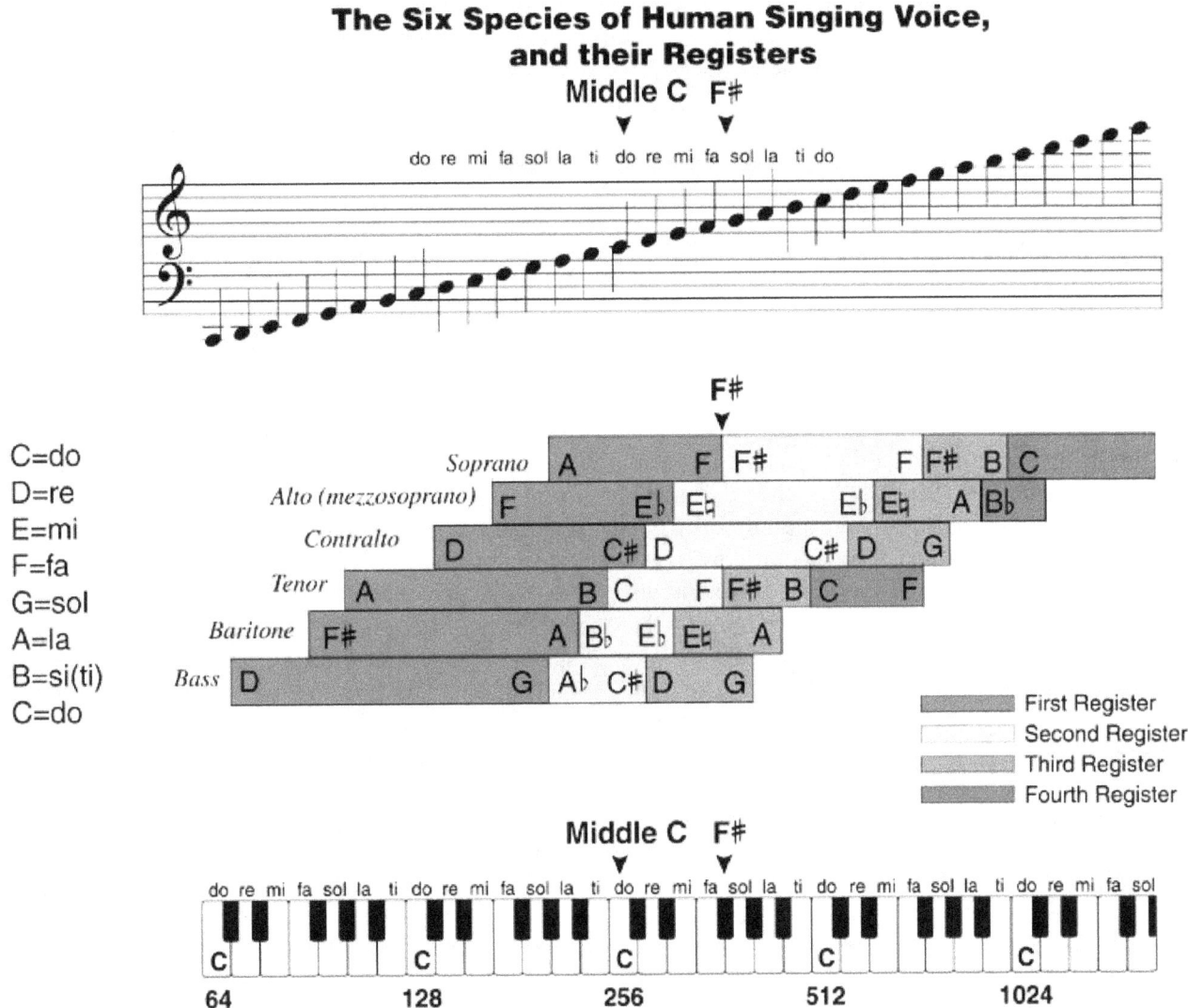

The Six Species of Human Singing Voice, and their Registers

C=do
D=re
E=mi
F=fa
G=sol
A=la
B=si(ti)
C=do

Manual on the Rudiments of Tuning and Registration, which is available for sale at www.schillerinstitute.org.

that Renata Tebaldi was pointing out, it wasn't only that high pitch makes singing high notes really hard, but that all of the notes are in the wrong place. That's something I think is an astonishing thing in itself, that these different types of voices, a tenor, a bass—it doesn't only mean you are higher or lower. Can you say anything about the internal characteristics of them?

Beets: Yes, briefly. Every human voice has a potential to be developed and trained according to what we refer to as the bel canto technique, which isn't just some method from Italy, from a long time ago. It's actually a method which recognizes the natural physiological potentials of the voice.

Each of what we call the species of voices—for example, in women there are sopranos, mezzosopranos, and contraltos—each of these voices themselves has natural areas of the voice which have different color characteristics. For example, the way in which a soprano will sing low notes versus high notes has to do with a different mixture of the resonance cavities, among other different things that you'll learn with vocal technique. Those changes from when the chest resonance is dominant, to the middle, then to where the head resonance is dominant— a singer doesn't just change whenever they feel like it. There are certain notes in the scale where for every soprano that shift naturally occurs. In certain very specific areas, she will pass from the middle to the higher resonances, and that is naturally determined.

When you start to raise the tuning pitch, you start to confuse the area in which that occurs, and it causes physiological strain on the voice. Additionally, for the music of somebody like Verdi, who composed with these different colors and qualities of the voices in mind, to give expression to the poetry, it messes up the poetry if you are shifting at the wrong place, whether it's a high note or a low note.

A Standard of Truth

Ross: You brought up truth in music, the existence of truth in culture, and using this as an example of the fact that if we can't maintain the standard of: "Hey, there is a standard of truth in this!", then look at all the other things this leads to more generally. You had mentioned in your introduction about how music wasn't only sounds. I was wondering if you could discuss at all about the unheard aspects of music—that the mind hears things that the ears don't. Sometimes there can even be a contrast between what the mind hears or expects versus what the notes indicate. Could you say anything about the substance of what music is?

Beets: There are a couple of ways I can try to get at it, briefly. First, I'd like to reference Furtwängler. Furtwängler lived in the terrible Twentieth Century, and conducted music in the midst of all the degeneration that was going on. Toward the end of his life he took to writing about music, not because he thought that was the best idea for a musician, but because the culture was becoming so ignorant of musical principles that he felt as if he had to write to try to express some of them. In his writings, he discusses an idea of a certain particular kind of tension that has to be present in any musical performance, and the tension he is discussing is the tension between the now, the moment that you are in, and the whole composition.

Imagine being a performer, even if you are not a musician, playing Beethoven's 5th Symphony. As you play, you're playing your notes and you're intoning the notes in a particular way. There is a certain causality of the moment of how you play, and how you move from note to note. That's in time, but there is something else which only comes into existence once the last note has sounded: the whole—the impression of the whole,

which doesn't exist completely in any particular part. It's this unity of the process of development which has occurred over the stretched-out time of all the moments.

Furtwängler discusses this tension, and that the musician is never only in one or only in the other. The musician is always experiencing how the moment is affecting what will eventually be the whole, and how his foreshadowing, his insight into the whole—which doesn't yet exist—affects the way in which he unfolds the moment. Now that's only possible with compositions which are actually expressions of real ideas, not just some stupid thing that you might hear on the radio today, some pop music. It's only true of compositions which actually intend to express a certain insight into the human mind, the human power of conceptualizing something universal about human beings, which is guiding every moment of that composition. Only things which are composed in that way are susceptible of it. Examples of that I mentioned are the works of Beethoven, also fugues of Bach are incredible from this standpoint, the sonatas of Mozart. LaRouche mentions quite often, and for good reason, Schubert's Ninth Symphony, and particularly Furtwängler's conducting of Schubert's Ninth Symphony.

Those things that I just attempted to describe, you don't hear those with your ears. You don't hear the tension between the moment and the whole with the ears, and yet that really is the principle which is determining the composition in its entirety, and which can be shared among many people with many sets of so-called ears. It's not in the sounds. It's something which is before and between the sounds.

Fan-Chiang: And it also very much assumes that there is something that is universal about the human mind and otherwise you wouldn't be able to say that I could write music that would move any human mind.

Beets: Exactly. It is accessible to any human mind, not accessible in the popular sense but in the same way a scientific discovery is accessible. I also want to mention, lest I gave the impression that this is something which died in 1989, that our organization has never let up the fight for the return to the lower tuning. In fact, we did a performance of Mozart's Requiem in 2014 in Boston in honor of John F. Kennedy at the lower tuning specifically, and made that a part of the intervention, so this is something which has continued and is a key part of our intervention into Manhattan now.

On the Employment of the Chorus in Tragedy

by Friedrich Schiller

*The following essay was translated by George W. Greg-
ory. It was originally published in the Schiller Institute's book* Friedrich Schiller/ Poet of Freedom, Volume
IV *in 2003. Subheads have been added.*

*This essay was written as the Prologue to Schiller's
tragedy,* The Bride of Messina, or, The Hostile Brothers,
*which was completed on February 1, 1803, and first
performed in the Weimar theater on March 19, 1803. In
writing this play, Schiller was influenced by his study of
the Classical Greek tragedies of Aeschylus and Sophocles, to reintroduce the ancient device of the chorus.*

A poetical work must justify itself, and where the
deed does not speak, words will not be to much avail.
One might well, therefore, leave it to the chorus to be its
own spokesman, were it for once given the appropriate
form of representation. But the tragic work of art first
becomes a whole in theatrical performance: the poet
only provides the words; music and dance must be added
to bring life to them. Thus, as long as the chorus lacks
this sensuously powerful accompaniment, it will appear
to be a thing extraneous to the economy of tragedy, a foreign body, and a way-station which only interrupts the
progress of the action, disturbs the illusion, and makes
the observer cold. To do justice to the chorus, therefore,
one must transpose oneself from the actual state to a possible one, but one must do that everywhere where one
intends to achieve something higher. That which art still
lacks, that it is to obtain; the fortuitous lack of resources
must not be permitted to constrain the creative power of
imagination of the poet. He sets himself the most worthy
as his goal, he strives toward an ideal, the practicing
artist may accommodate himself to the circumstances.

It is not true, as one usually hears the claim made,
that the audience degrades art; the artist degrades the
audience, and at all times when art degenerated, it fell
because of the artists. The audience needs nothing more
than receptivity, and this it possesses. It steps before the
curtain with an indeterminate yearning, with a manifold

capacity. Among the highest of these, it brings an ability, it takes pleasure in what is intelligent and right, and
if it once begins to be satisfied with what is bad, it will
assuredly cease to demand what is excellent, even when
it is provided.

The poet, one hears the objection, does well to work
according to an ideal, the art critic does well to judge
according to ideas, contingent, limited, practicing art
rests upon satisfying the wants to others. The entrepre-
neur wants to continue to exist, the actor wants to show
himself, the audience wants to be entertained and
moved. The audience seeks enjoyment, and is dissatis-
fied if one demands an effort from it, where it expected
a play and recreation.

But by treating theater more seriously, one does not
want to do away with the enjoyment of the audience,
but to ennoble it. It should remain a play, but a poetical
one. All art is dedicated to joy, and there is no higher
and no more serious task than to make people happy.
True art is only that art which provides the highest enjoyment. Supreme enjoyment is the freedom of the
mind in the living play of all of its powers.

True art—Achieving Liberation

Every person, indeed, expects from the arts of imagination a certain liberation from the bounds of the real
world; he wants to take pleasure in what is possible and
give room to his own phantasy. He who sets his expectations the lowest, still wants to forget his business, his
common life, his particular individuality, he wants to
feel himself in extraordinary situations, he wants to delight in the strange combinations of chance; if he is of a
more serious nature, he wants to find the moral world-
government, which he misses in real life, upon the
stage. But he himself knows quite well, that he is en-
gaging in but an empty play, that in fact he takes delight
only in dreams, and when he returns from the theater
back to the real world, it will surround him once more
with its full, oppressive constriction; he is its booty as

An illustration of Friedrich Schiller's tragedy The Bride of Messina, from Project Gutenberg at the Berlin State Library.

he was before, and it has not been changed in the slightest. Thus, nothing but a pleasant delusion of the moment has been won, which disappears when one awakens.

And just for that reason, because the intent here is but a temporary illusion, all that is necessary is thus but an appearance of truth, or popular probability, which one so gladly sets in the place of truth.

True art, however, does not aim merely at a temporary play; it seriously intends not to transpose a person into a merely momentary dream of freedom, but to make him really and in fact free, and to accomplish this by awakening in him a force, exercising it and developing it, to thrust the sensuous world, which otherwise only presses upon us as crude material, bearing down upon us as a blind power, into an objective distance, to transpose it into a free work of our mind, and to achieve mastery over the material with ideas.

And just for that reason, because true art wants something real and objective, it cannot be satisfied

merely with the appearance of truth; upon the truth itself, upon the firm and deep foundation of nature, art erects its ideal edifice.

But now, how art can be at once entirely ideal and yet in the most profound sense real—how it can take leave utterly from what is real and yet be in most precise accord with nature, that is what few comprehend, which makes the view of poetic and plastic works so furtive, because these two requirements seem to cancel each other out in the common way of judging.

Furthermore, it usually happens that one seeks to achieve the first by sacrificing the other, and fails to meet either requirement for that very reason. He who is endowed by nature with a true sense and an intimacy of emotion, but who is deprived of creative imagination, will be a faithful painter of reality; he will be able to grasp chance phenomena, but never the spirit of nature. He will restore the material of nature to us, but it does not become our work on that account, not the free product of our forming mind, and can thus also not have the beneficial effect of art, which consists in freedom. Such an artist and poet will leave us in a serious mood, but distasteful, and we shall see ourselves painfully thrown back into the mean narrowness of reality by the very art which should have liberated us. On the other hand, he who partakes indeed of a vivid imagination, but without mind and character, will not trouble himself over any truth; he will, instead, but play with the material of the world, will only seek to surprise us with fantastical and bizarre constructions, and since everything he does is only foam and fancy, he will, to be sure, entertain us for the moment, but he will neither build nor found anything in the mind. His play, like the seriousness of the other, is not poetical. To arrange fantastic portraits in an arbitrary sequence does not mean entering into the ideal, and to present reality imitatively does not signify a representation of nature. These two requirements are so little in contradiction with each other that they are, instead, one and the same: art is for that reason true, that it completely takes leave of reality and becomes purely ideal. Nature herself is only an idea of the mind, which never impinges upon the senses. She lies beneath the blanket of appearances, but never appears herself. It is granted alone to the art of the ideal, or actually it is her mission, to grasp this mind of the universe, and bind it to a corporeal form. Even this art cannot present the universe to the senses, but yet, by means of her creating force, she can present it to the power of imagination, and on that account be more true than all reality, and more real than all experience. It follows, self-evidently, that the artist can use no single element of reality as he finds it, that his work must be ideal in all of its parts, if it is to have reality as a whole and be in agreement with nature.

What is true of poetry and art as a whole, also holds for all of the species of the same, and what has just been said, may be applied to tragedy with no difficulty. Here, too, one has struggled for a long time, and is still struggling, with the common notion of natural, which as much as annuls and destroys all poetry and art. The plastic arts are grudgingly conceded a certain ideality, more out of convention and for internal reasons, but from poetry and the dramatic arts, in particular, one demands illusion, which, were it actually achievable, would only be the miserable fraud of a pick-pocket. Everything external in a dramatic performance is contrary to this notion—everything is but a symbol of reality. The very day in the theater is only artificial, the architecture is only symbolic, the metrical language itself is ideal, but the action is supposed to be real, and the part destroys the whole. The French, who first misunderstood the spirit of the ancients, thus introduced a unity of place and time in the crudest empirical sense upon the stage, as if this were a place different from merely ideal space, and a time different from the mere continuous succession of the action.

One has come a large step closer to poetical tragedy by introducing metrical speech. Some lyrical experiments on the stage have been successful, and, in individual cases, poetry has carried a number of victories over dominant prejudice by virtue of its own vital force. But little is won in these individual cases, if the error is not felled in the whole, and it is not sufficient that only that is tolerated as poetic freedom, which is in fact the essence of all poetry. The introduction of the chorus were the last, the crowning step; and if it only served to openly and honestly declare war upon naturalism in art; to us it should be a living wall which tragedy draws around itself in order to close itself off completely from the real world, and to maintain for itself its ideal ground, its poetic freedom.

Enter the Chorus

The tragedy of the Greeks, as we know, emerged from the chorus. And although it cut itself loose from the chorus historically and in the course of time, one can also say that it emerged from the chorus poetically and in spirit, and that without this perseverent witness

and bearer of the action, it would have become an entirely different poetry. The dissolution of the chorus, and drawing this sensuously powerful organ together into the characterless, boring, ever returning figure of a miserable confidant, was thus no such great improvement of the tragedy, as the French and those who parrot them have imagined.

Ancient tragedy, which initially dealt only with gods, heroes, and kings, required the chorus as a necessary accompaniment; it found it in nature, and employed it because it found it. The actions and fates of the heroes and kings are public in and of themselves, and were even more so in simple, primal time. The chorus, thus, was more than a natural organ in ancient tragedy; it followed out of the poetical form of real life. In modern tragedy, it becomes an artificial organ, it helps to bring poetry forth. The modern poet no longer finds the chorus in nature; he must create it poetically and introduce it, i.e., he must make such a change in the story he treats, whereby it is transposed into that childlike time and that simple form of life.

For the modern poet, therefore, the chorus performs a far more essential service than it did for the ancient poet, and just for the very reason that it transforms the common modern world into the ancient poetical one, because it makes everything useless which contends against poetry, and drives him aloft to the most simple, the most original, and most naive motifs. The palace of the kings is now closed; the courts have withdrawn from the gates of the city into the inner courts of the buildings; writing has displaced the living word;, the people itself, the sensuous, living mass, where it does not make itself felt as raw power, has become the state, and thus become a derivative conception; the gods have returned within the breasts of people. The poet must open the palaces once again; he must conduct the courts out under the open heavens; he must resurrect the gods; he must reestablish everything immediate, which has been annulled by the artificial edifice of real life; and he must cast off all artificial concoctions of the person and around him, everything which hinders the appearance of his inner nature and his original character, as a sculptor casts off modern robes, and he must take nothing of the external environment except that which makes the highest of forms, the human form, visible.

But just as the plastic artist spreads the pleated fullness of robes about his figures in order to fill the space of his portrait richly and gracefully, combining the disparate parts in a continuity of calm masses, giving the color, which entices and pleases the eye, room to play, ingeniously veiling the human form and making it visible at the same time, in the same way the tragic poet carries through and surrounds his rigorously proportioned action and the firm contours of his acting figures with a lyrical, splendid fabric, in which the acting persons, as if in a broadly folded robe of purple, move freely and nobly with dignity and high composure.

In a higher organization, the material or the elementary need no longer be visible, the chemical color disappears in the fine carnation

The chorus in a production of Sophocles' tragedy Antigone.

of a living being. But the material, too, has its splendor, and can, as such, be taken up in a work of art. But then it must earn its place with life and fullness, and with harmony, and it must vindicate the forms which it surrounds, rather than suffocate them with its gravity.

This is easy for everyone to understand in works of the plastic arts, but the same happens in poetry, and in the tragical, which is the subject of our attention here. Everything which the understanding expresses, in general, is like that which merely excites the senses, only material and raw element in a poetic work, and where it predominates, it will inevitably destroy the poetical, because it lies at the point of indifference of the ideal and the sensuous. Now, the human being is so constituted, that he always wants to proceed from the particular to the universal, and therefore reflection must also have its place in tragedy. But if it is to earn this place, it must obtain that through the presentation which it lacks in sensuous life, since if the two elements of poetry, the ideal and the sensuous, are to work in intimate connection together, then they must work beside one another, or the poetry is annulled. If the scale does not stand perfectly still, the balance can only be established by an oscillation of the two pans of the scale.

And this is the function of the chorus in tragedy. The chorus itself is not an individual, rather a general conception, but this conception represents itself in a sensuous, powerful mass, which impresses the senses with its opulent presence. The chorus leaves the narrow arena of the action, in order to make statements about the past and future, about distant times and peoples, about what is human in general, to draw the grand results of life and to express the teachings of wisdom. But it does this with the full power of fantasy, with a bold lyrical freedom, which coincides, at the high summit of things human, as though with the stride of the gods—and it does this accompanied by the full sensuous power of rhythm and music, in sound and movement.

The chorus thus purifies the tragic poem by segregating reflection from the action, and equips itself with poetic power by means of this segregation, just as the plastic artist transforms the common requirement of clothing into charm and beauty with rich draperies.

Lifting Up the Mind

But just as the painter sees himself compelled to intensify the color-tone of the living being to maintain the balance of powerful materials, the lyrical speech of the chorus compels the poet to proportionally elevate the entire speech of the poem, and thus to intensify the sensuous power of the expression in general. Only the chorus justifies the tragic poet in this exaltation of tone which fills the ear, enraptures the spirit, expands the entire mind. This, a gigantic form in his portrait, compels him to place all of his characters upon the cothurnus, thereby giving his portrait tragic magnitude. If the chorus is removed, the language of tragedy must be lowered on the whole, or that which is grand and powerful will seem forced and exaggerated. To introduce the ancient chorus into French tragedy would reveal it in its full paltriness and destroy it; without any doubt, introducing it into Shakespeare's tragedy would reveal its true significance for the first time.

While the chorus brings life to the speech, it brings calm to the action—but the beautiful and high calm which must be the character of a noble work of art. The mind of the audience must maintain its freedom even amidst the fiercest passion, it should not fall prey to impressions, rather take its leave of the emotions which it suffers, always clear and bright. What the usual judgment tends to fault about the chorus, that it dissolves the illusion, that it breaks the force of the affects, is actually its highest recommendation, for it is this very blind force of affects which the true artist avoids, it is this illusion which he disdains to excite. If the blows with which tragedy strikes our heart were to follow one another without interruption, suffering would vanquish activity. We would be immersed in the material, and no longer hover over it. By holding the parts apart, and stepping between the passions with its calming reflection, it restores our freedom to us, which would be lost in the storm of affects. The tragic characters also require this place of repose, this calm, in order to collect themselves, for they are no real beings, which obey merely the force of the moment, rather ideal persons and representatives of their species, which express the depth of humanity. The presence of the chorus, which listens to them as a judging witness, and harnesses the first outbreak of their passion with its intervention, motivates the presence of mind with which they act, and the dignity with which they speak. They stand, to a degree, upon a natural theater, because they speak and act in front of observers, and they will therefore speak all the more fittingly from the artificial theater to its audience.

So much on the subject of my right to reintroduce the ancient chorus upon the tragic stage. Choruses are, indeed, already known in modern tragedy, but the chorus of Greek tragedy, the way I have employed it here, the chorus as a single ideal person, which carries the entire action and accompanies it, this is fundamentally different from that opera-like chorus, and if I now and then hear talk about Greek choruses instead of a chorus, I become suspicious that someone does not know what he is talking about. The chorus of ancient tragedy, to my knowledge, has not appeared on the stage since the demise of the same.

I have indeed separated the chorus into two parts, and represented it in conflict with itself; but this is only the case where it joins in the action as a real person and as a blind mass. As chorus and as ideal person, it is always identical with itself. I have changed the place and allowed the chorus to exit a number of times; but Aeschylus, too, the creator of tragedy, and Sophocles, the great master in this art, also employed this liberty.

Another liberty I have permitted myself, may be more difficult to justify. I have employed the Christian religion and the Greek gods together, and even recalled the faith of the Moors. But the location of the play is Messina, where these three religions still express themselves, partly in living form, partly in monuments, and they speak to the senses. And I hold it to be a right of poetry to treat the different religions as a collective whole for the power of imagination, in which everything which has its own character, expresses its own sensibility, has its place. Beneath the shroud of all religions there lies religion itself, the idea of one divinity, and it must be permitted to the poet to express this in whichever form he finds most comfortable and most fitting.

'All Men Become Brothers': The Decades-Long Struggle for Beethoven's Ninth Symphony

by Michelle Rasmussen

When Germany, and the world, celebrated the 25th anniversary of the fall of the Berlin Wall on Nov. 9, 2014, as in 1989, there was no better way to express the joy of freedom, than by a performance of Beethoven's 9th Symphony.

Beethoven, drawing on Friedrich Schiller, the great poet of freedom, gave us a gift, not only for German speakers, but for all humanity. And, as pointed out by Lyndon LaRouche, to compose such a gift, it is not the love of music, but the love of humanity, which is the source of the passion the musician, no, the human being, draws from. Beethoven, himself, wrote that his call was "to use my art as a means of relieving needy humanity."

Yes, it is out of this passion, pouring out in tones, that the human moves his fellow men and women to look inside themselves, to find their own fount of creativity, compassion, and yearning to make an immortal contribution to all of humanity.

Let us begin our story at the end, and let us end at the beginning.

Listening in retrospect, you can partake in the future yet to be.

...God, like one of our own architects, approached the task of constructing the universe with order and pattern, and laid out the individual parts accordingly, as if it were not art which imitated Nature, but God himself had looked to the mode of building of Man who was to be.

— Johannes Kepler
Mysterium Cosmographicum

Let us begin with Beethoven's 9th Symphony, which ends with a surprise—human voices intoning the ideas of Friedrich Schiller's poem, *Ode to Joy*, intertwined with orchestral voices, to create one of the most moving works of art in history.

Then, let us reverse time, and go back through Beethoven's thirty year-long quest to accomplish this, stopping alongside some of the musical milestones which led to this immortal masterpiece, conscious of the fact that we can only listen to these precursors, with the tones of their successors ringing in our ears. We will take LaRouche's concept of time reversal—that the future determines, and changes, the past—and see how that applies to music.

Ludwig van Beethoven

Time node F: 1824: The 9th Symphony

Rarely in human history has there been a dialogue and synthesis of two great minds on the level of Friedrich Schiller and Ludwig van Beethoven, although they never met. The result was the 9th Symphony.

The reader is urged to listen to two versions of the 9th Symphony, especially the fourth choral movement. First, to a performance with the great German conductor Wilhelm Furtwängler,[1] and then to a performance by the Schiller Institute's European chorus.[2]

Near-Hearing and Far-Hearing

In 1824, Beethoven made a musical revolution by weaving Friedrich Schiller's poem *An die Freude* (The Ode to Joy) into the 4th movement of his 9th Symphony. In so doing, Beethoven created a sublime unity of effect both within the fourth movement, and, because he musically quotes from the previous three movements, the entire symphony.

The symphony is a good example of musical time reversal in a single masterpiece—playing with time, backwards and forwards—where the unfolding of the music, as it is being performed, is driven by the concept of the future, completed unity, which is present, at all times, in the minds of the conductor, such as Furtwängler, the musicians, and the listeners.

Furtwängler self-consciously named this phenomenon. He described it as the tension between the "Nahören" (near-hearing), the music that is being heard right now, and the "Fernhören" (far-hearing), the future, unified, completed musical idea. The two intersect at every moment, and the tension between listening to the present from the future, and the future from the present, is what gives the composition, as it is being performed, its gripping, driving quality, creating a "dynamic quality of musical space-time."[3]

Beethoven was also self-conscious of this when composing. "[M]y custom when I am composing even instrumental music is always to keep the whole before my eyes,"[4] and work towards realizing it. He once made a note to himself to sketch out all of the voices as they appeared in his mind, not only the theme, to get accustomed, at once, to the concept of the whole.

In the 9th Symphony, he achieved this unity of effect, spanning crisscrossing directions of time, by bringing the listener along a journey of discovery. He searches for a theme capable of expressing Joy—"Freude"— introduces a lone human voice just at the transition from searching to finding, and then, causes that simple theme to appear as a leading character, as one of several voices (polyphony), constantly undergoing contrapuntal development, by crafting a succession of variations, unceasingly driving toward the last variation in the future, but, simultaneously, always reflecting backwards to the first appearance of the *Freude* theme, and always having the development process that led to the theme, in the mind's eye.

In preparation for investigating how Beethoven plays with time in the 4th movement, let us pause to consider the crucial aspect of Beethoven's creative genius—the non-linear development within his compositions, from one section to another, driven by a specific driving, unifying principle of musical change.

Non-Linear Increase in Creativity

Back in 1977, Lyndon LaRouche addressed the question of Beethoven's creative process, and how playing, or listening to, Beethoven's music was the most conducive method of preparing your own mind to do creative work.[5]

The key to discovering Beethoven's creativity is to consider him one of the greatest scientific minds in human history. Look at each of his compositions as part of a process of musical self-development. They are stepping stones along a journey which, taken as a whole, becomes "a process of fundamental, epistemologically ordered discoveries."[6]

That is, view each of Beethoven's compositions as a new scientific discovery, within a process of leaping (by hops, not straight-lined linear motion) toward more and more profound, revolutionary discoveries.

Then, view the development within a single composition as a series of discoveries, generated by one subsuming discovery, which generates the others.

The measuring rod for musical progress in, espe-

1. Performed 1954, Luzerne Festival.

2. http://www.schillerinstitute.org/music/2010/beethoven_9th_berlin_c256.html

3. EIR, Vol. 39, No. 24.

4. Stated while composing his opera *Fidelio*, fn. 49 in Solomon, Maynard, "Reason and Imagination: Beethoven's Aesthetic Evolution," essay in *Beethoven Essays*, University of California Press, 2003, p. 98.

5. The Secret of Ludwig van Beethoven.

6. The study of the nature and basis of knowledge.

cially, Beethoven's late works, is not fixed, but changes, non-linearly, based on the increasing quality, or density, of development in the next section. Thus, the measuring rod, or to put it another way, Beethoven's own creative power, is, itself, constantly changing, and he demands that ours does too.[7]

Beethoven, more than any other composer, made insights into his own creativity, as expressed in his compositions, the subject of his musical consciousness, thus forming his "self-consciously Promethean identity as a musician."[8]

Therefore, when we listen to Beethoven's works, when we envelop ourselves in his creative genius, he can teach us how to be creative ourselves, as Prometheus gave fire and the power of creativity to mankind, enabling us to create something new to pass on to future generations.

Listening to Beethoven's music, really listening, and partaking in his journey of discovery, then, is the most intensive mental activity you can have.

LaRouche even let us in on a secret—being delighted by the way Beethoven surprised him, being drawn into the driving quality of the development of the music, the progress from one phase of development to the next, created the best intellectual climate for his own creative work.

The Evolution of an Idea

As we will see, after thinking about how to express the central idea in the *Ode to Joy* in music since at least 1794, Beethoven had come to the conclusion that only the combination of a full orchestra, chorus, and soloists, would be powerful enough to elevate Schiller's ideas even higher than in the poem.

He had penned words from Schiller's *An die Freude* amongst his 1812 sketches for the 7th and 8th Symphonies: "*Freude schöner Götterfunken Tochter*—work

FIGURE 1

out the overture." Two pages later, the following themes and motives were found. (**Figures 1 and 2**)[9] Beethoven would use two of these themes in his 1815 overture Zur Namensfeier (Name Day), op. 115, although he did not include Schiller's Ode.[10]

Beethoven considered different plans for new sym-

---

7. "Instead of imagining space-time as measuring displacements according to a fixed reference-scale, imagine that forward displacements of a space-time-matter continuum change the ostensibly linear scales employed for the preceding moment. Imagine that this change in the basis-measurement is of such a form that instead of measuring displacement of the developing continuum according to linear (scalar) magnitudes of increments of time, distance, mass-energy, and so forth, that the scale of measurement is a series of numbers determined by an exponential function. That is perhaps the best heuristic representation of the general idea for today's ordinary informed consciousness. It also expresses precisely the consequence of Beethoven's approach to composition in the late quartets and related works." LaRouche, *op. cit.*

8. LaRouche, Lyndon, *The Florestan Principle in Art*, 1977, The Schiller Institute at: http://www.schillerinstitute.org/music/2010/lyn_florestan_principle.html

---

9. "Fürsten sind Bettler." "Princes are beggars"! John Sigerson, the Schiller Institute's musical director, pointed out that it's amazing that Beethoven didn't get thrown into prison for writing that, showing how much he was protected by certain powerful circles in Vienna.

10. It was supposed to be performed on the name day of Austrian Emperor Franz I, as a patriotic celebration after the downfall of Napoleon, who had occupied Vienna while Beethoven lived there. "The poetical idea of the work was not essentially changed—the joy of liberated Europe simply taking the place of the joy of Schiller's poem," wrote Beethoven biographer Thayer. Beethoven shared Schiller's deeply felt longing for political freedom. Beethoven's motto was: "To do good whenever one can, to love liberty above all else, never to deny the truth, even though it be before the throne," written in 1793. "Wohltunen, wo man kann;/Freiheit über alles lieben;/Wahrheit nie, auch sogar am/Throne, nicht verleugnen. Krogh, Torben and Berg." Sigurd, *Beethovens 9. Symfoni, Rosenkilde og Baggers Forlag*, Copenhagen, 1949. English translation: http://www.worldofquotes.com/author/Beethoven/1/

FIGURE 2

FIGURE 3

phonies. One was a symphony where one movement would make use of the human voice to unite Greek mythology and old church song, written in an ancient mode. Another plan was for a four-movement symphony, with a musical setting of Schiller's poem as the finale.

After the 8th Symphony, Beethoven decided to do just that in a German Symphony (Symphony Allemande). But then, he changed his mind, and would use Schiller's poem as the text for the sublime last movement of the four-movement symphony in D he had been writing.[11] Beethoven would later transform the original fourth movement into becoming the finale of String Quartet op. 132.[12]

Beethoven left a sketch of his search for a basic hymn for the poem, changing the melody and rhythm until he wrote, "This is it. Ha, now it is found," and, then, "Freude, schöner" underneath the final theme. (**Figure 3**)

But how was he to make a transition to the poem? There were hardly any precedents, as the human voice had only been heard twice before in a symphony. Beethoven came up with the idea of musically quoting from each of the first three movements, repeating the same dissonant chords heard in the beginning of the movement, and then having the bass sing: "Oh friends, not these tones. Instead, let us raise our voices in more pleasing, more joyful sounds. Joy!"[13]

In the midst of the creative tension surrounding how to introduce

11. Thayer reports that the first three movements were already written, but Jan Swafford in his new biography *Beethoven*, argues that Beethoven wrote the first three movements with the new last movement in mind.

12. Bonnie Koo, Symphony with Final Chorus on Schiller's "Ode to Joy," Classical Net, 1997.

13. Alexander, Ian from https://www.youtube.com/watch?v=4pbMUEHvoAo

the choral section, Beethoven wrote in the margin:

"Lasst uns das Lied des unsterblichen Schillers singen, Freude, etc." ("Let us sing the words of the immortal Schiller, Joy, etc.")[14]

He would use the version of the poem as amended by Schiller in 1803, selecting only certain sections, reorganized by Beethoven's own ordering principle. The multi-faceted reflections of Joy, brought forth by love, form a progressive manifold, generally ascending higher and higher from the terrestrial to the celestial—in nature, love between man and woman, brotherly love, and God's love.[15] (See box for text)

For both Schiller and Beethoven, Joy (*Freude*) was inseparably linked to Freedom (*Freiheit*). Although Beethoven would call forth Schiller's message of brotherly love, or universal brotherhood, in 1824, as a powerful manifestation for political freedom for humanity, against the repressive police state which Prince Metternich had been constructing after the 1815 Congress of Vienna, his masterpiece would be timeless.[16]

In 1942, while Denmark was under the yoke of the Nazi

---

14. In October 1823, Beethoven's friend Schindler wrote, "One day he burst into the room and shouted at me: 'I got it! I have it!' He held his sketchbook out to me so that I could read: "Let us sing the song of the immortal Schiller"; then a solo voice began the hymn of joy." (Plantiga, 64)

15. Bonnie Koo, Symphony with Final Chorus on Schiller's "Ode to Joy", Classical Net, 1997.

16. Sachs, Harvey, review of his book *The Ninth: Beethoven and the World in 1824*.

An Die Freude

Freude, schöner Götterfunken,
Tochter aus Elysium,
Wir betreten feuertrunken,
Himmlische dein Heiligtum.
Deine Zauber binden wieder,
Was die Mode streng geteilt;
Alle Menschen werden Brüder,[1]
Wo dein sanfter Flügel weilt.

Wem der grosse Wurf gelungen,
Eines Freundes Freund zu sein,
Wer ein holdes Weib errungen,
Mische seine Jubel ein!
Ja—wer auch nur eine Seele
Sein nennt auf dem Erdenrund!
Und wer's nie gekonnt, der stehle
Weinend sich aus diesem Bund!

Freude trinken alle Wesen
An den Brüsten der Natur,
Alle Guten, alle Bösen
Folgen ihre Rosenspur.
Küsse gab sie uns und Reben,
Einen Freund, geprueft im Tod,
Wollust ward dem Wurm gegeben,
Und der Cherub steht vor Gott!

Froh, wie seine Sonnen fliegen
Durch das Himmels praecht'gen
    Plan,
Laufet, Brüder, eure Bahn,
Freudig wie ein Held zum Siegen.

Seid umschlungen, Millionen!
Diesen Kuss der ganzen Welt!
Brüder—überm Sternenzelt
Muss ein lieber Vater wohnen.
Ihr stürzt nieder, Millionen?
Ahnest du den Schöpfer, Welt?
Such ihn überm Sternenzelt,
Über Sternen muss er wohnen.

---

1. Schiller's original 1785 version for these two lines read:
Was der Mode Schwert geteilt
Bettler werden Fürstenbrueder.

Ode to Joy

Joy, thou beauteous godly lightning,
Daughter of Elysium,
Fire drunken we are ent'ring
Heavenly, thy holy home!
Thy enchantments bind together,
What did custom stern divide
Every man becomes a brother,[2]
Where thy gentle wings abide.

Who the noble prize achieveth,
Good friend of a friend to be;
Who a lovely wife attaineth,
Join us in his jubilee!
Yes—he too who but one being
On this earth can call his own!
He who ne'er was able, weeping
Stealeth from this league alone!

Joy is drunk by every being
From kind nature's flowing breasts,
Every evil, every good thing
For her rosy footprint quests.
Gave she us both vines and kisses,
In the face of death, a friend,
To the worm were given blisses
And the Cherubs God attend.

As the suns are flying, happy
Through the heaven's glorious
    plane,
Travel, brothers, down your lane,
Joyful as in hero's vict'ry.

Be embrac'd, ye million yonder!
Take this kiss throughout the world!
Brothers—o'er the stars unfurl'd
Must reside a loving father.
Fall before him, all ye millions?
Know'st thou the Creator, world?
Seek above the stars unfurl'd,
Yonder dwells he in the heavens.[3]

---

2. Schiller's original 1785 version for these two lines read:
What custom's sword divide
Beggars are a prince's brother.

3. See the Wertz' translation of the entire poem.

occupation, Rudolf Simonsen, rector of The Royal Music Conservatory in Copenhagen, in his book, *Sub Specie Æternitatis*, about musical masterpieces considered from the standpoint of eternity, concluded his chapter about Beethoven's 9th thusly:

> The great line in music only goes through that music which contains greatness. In the eternal world—there from which the greatest in art brings tidings—every person is entwined in a common bond of love. 'Alle Menschen werden Brüder'—Yes, that Beethoven was drawn by the greatness of these words, you will be able to understand, when you first understand his own greatness. The 9th, in particular, one of the most distinctive art works of all times, sets no limits, but embraces everything and everyone; it preaches something common, something universal, something eternal: the sublime Gospel of the power of man, and human love."[17]

The Battle Plan

Beethoven musters all resources available for his gigantic challenge—to write a work where the voices that sing Schiller's ideas could be contrapuntally[18] woven together with voices from the orchestra, to crown the climax of the entire symphony.

This is not an Ode to Joy anthem with orchestral accompaniment. The singing voices become an integral part of what is, perhaps, the most driving contrapuntal development in all history. Beethoven's contrapuntal ironies and surprises must shine through.[19]

Beethoven is constantly interchanging between different sections of the orchestra, the full orchestra, and the orchestra with single soloists, a group of four soloists, and the entire chorus.

The Joy-theme variations develop through the use of different counterpoint voices, different rhythms, the entrance of a second theme which leads to the highpoint of the movement—a double-fugue[20] between the Joy-

theme and the second theme, bookended by two special sections, all of which culminates in a joyous grand finale.

Actually, LaRouche asks us to look at the entire movement as being governed by the late Beethoven principle of the double fugue, even from the standpoint of the Grosse Fugue, Op. 133-134—as a Grosse Fugue for orchestra and voice.

Here is a short overview of the battle plan:

Beethoven began the fourth movement with an astounding entrance, filled with orchestral dissonances—Chaos! Where are we?

The search begins for music capable of expressing the essence of Schiller's poem— especially that single word Joy, *Freude,* which, as stated above, is linked to the word Freedom, *Freiheit,* as the joy derived from the freedom of musical development also underlies. LaRouche sees this *Freude/Freiheit* interrelationship as a generative principle of development.

The cellos and basses lead the search through instrumental recitatives, which Beethoven said should be played as if there were words underneath the notes—a foreshadow of the human singing that is to come in the future. They are interspersed with musical quotes from each of the first three movements from the past, cast aside in turn, because they are inadequate to express Joy.[21]

Then, out of this musical wandering, this seeking, and not finding, a simple, folk-song-like theme emerges, which Beethoven will later integrate into an anti-entropic, that is, more ordered, more developed, series of variations.

After a couple of tentative attempts, the variation-journey begins with the softest, deepest, unisonal tones of the cellos and double basses, as if from the shadows, at first, a "song without words," sung by the same instruments which were searching before. The unisonal is then superseded by the contrapuntal. A series of three beautiful, polyphonic variations ensues, with more and more instrumental voices in play, and, therefore, increasingly intensive contrapuntal development.

After another dissonant disturbance, harkening back to the very beginning of the movement, Beethoven

17. Simonsen, Rudolf, *Sub Specie Æternitatis*, Wilhelm Hansen, Copenhagen, 1942, page 155. Translated from the Danish by this author.

18. The art of weaving several independent voices together into a whole, dynamically changing, musical fabric.

19. LaRouche, Lyndon, "The Secret of Ludwig van Beethoven," *op. cit.*

20. A fugue, taken from the Italian word "to hunt," is the name of a piece of music where a short musical motif, called the subject, first appears alone, and then, in turn, as the other voices enter, in succession, as

if they are chasing each other. A double fugue is when, not one, but two fugal subjects are employed, as counterpoint to each other. This makes the contrapuntal development doubly intensive.

21. Maybe this condensation of time, is what led LaRouche to assert that the transitional bass recitative section superseded Bach's fugal stretto. A stretto, from the Italian for narrow or close, is when fugal entrances start before they had previously, overlapping each other, causing a condensation of time, and an intensification of effect.

The Christmas Eve 1989 performance of Beethoven's Ninth Symphony, played in the center of Berlin to celebrate the fall of the Berlin Wall.

makes his revolutionary non-linear upward jump—the instrumental recitative from before, is now superseded by the startling entrance of a human voice, in the middle of a symphony! In the transcendental passage mentioned above, the lone baritone, in the same tonal range as the cellos and basses, starting with the beginning notes from the first instrumental recitative, and ending with the same notes as the last instrumental recitative, first rejects the past, and then reaches for the future, through his embrace of the Joy theme, this time, a song with words.

"The joining of Schiller's poem and Beethoven's tones is unspeakably liberating; it is as if everything in us is expanded through the noble, which expanded the minds of the two great ones. This is not just a question of music, but about the infinite, of which music is a part," as Rudolf Simonsen expressed it.[22]

And now, yet another revolutionary leap— an entire chorus joins in! As the next two stanzas of the poem proceed, the four soloists take their turn in the variations.

At the culmination of the rising tones, on the words "vor Gott," "[standing] before God," with the tension held as long as possible, it is "as if the gate of Heaven explodes, and we sink back stunned."[23]

Out of the silence, a rhythmically vibrant victory march emerges, sung by a soldier and his comrades, leading into a battling double-fugal orchestral variation based on two variations of the theme, which foreshadows the choral double-fugue to come. This is followed by the chorus at full throttle.

Then, there is a dramatic shift, and a second theme enters when the male choristers sing the words "Seid umschlungen, Millionen! Diesen Kuss der ganzen Welt!" "Be embrac'd, ye millions yonder! Take this kiss throughout the world!" Simonsen writes, "The hymn is for the entirety of humanity: no limits are drawn; all, all are included in the great community."[24]

The intensity increases as Beethoven leads us to two deeply moving, ethereal sections, where humanity seeks a loving God beyond the heavens, serving as spiritual paths climbing up to, and down from the summit—a double-fugal interweaving of the two themes from the past— the main "Freude schöner Götterfunken," Joy theme, and the second theme on "Seid Umschlungen, Millionen!"[25]

The soloists, with orchestral accompaniment, return to intone sections of the beginning text, in yet another variation, reaching a highpoint on "Alle Menschen werden Brüder," "All men become brothers,"[26] underscored by the chorus, leading to the final variation of the "Seid umschlungen" theme, with full chorus and orchestra, shifting into both a very loud fortissimo, and a very fast tempo.

The symphony concludes in jubilation, as it began, with "Freude schöner Götterfunken, Götterfunken."

---

22. Simonsen, *op. cit.*, page 152.
23. *Ibid.*

24. *Ibid*, page 153.
25. Listen to the video by Fred Haight from the LaRouche movement: "How Beethoven Thinks: The Double Fugue in the Ode to Joy!"
26. Where Joy's gentle wings wave.

With the completion of the 9th Symphony, Beethoven finally succeeded in his long quest, drawing deeply from his passionate love of humanity, and creative spirit, to create a masterpiece that has inspired feeling souls in every generation since—around the world from Japan, where it is played every year to celebrate New Year; to China; to its birthplace in Germany, when the people wanted to express their unbounded joy after the fall of the Berlin Wall. Even conductor Leonard Bernstein was swept up by the historical moment, and chose to replace "Freude" by "Freiheit" (freedom).

Beethoven as a young man.

Even if Beethoven had only written this one piece, he would be immortal—but, of course, that would be impossible without the "small steps and giant leaps" he had taken beforehand.

As Furtwängler wrote, "The 9th Symphony is surely the end and the crowning of all Beethoven Symphonies. …. The 9th Symphony belonged, according to Beethoven, to the great works of his last period, together with the Missa Solemnis, the last sonatas and the quartets."

In hindsight, Beethoven considered his "Choral Fantasy" as an introductory study to the 9th Symphony. In submitting the Symphony to a publisher, Beethoven wrote that it was:

"… a major new symphony, which has a finale with the entrance of vocal solo[s] and chorus, to the words of Schiller's immortal song, An die Freude, similar to my Choral Fantasy, with chorus, but far greater."

Now, imagine going back in time, as a spaceship moves through the stars—with the numbers for Beethoven's age, and some dates, interspersed with musical notes flying by, stopping at age 38.

Time node E: 1808: The Choral Fantasy

Beethoven would hold an Academy—a grand 4-hour-long concert consisting of the premiers of the 5th and 6th Symphonies, the fourth piano concerto, and sections of the Mass in C. But just as a great symphony has a great finale, how would he conclude this great evening?

Then Beethoven got the idea to unite the full orchestra, chorus and soloists in an homage to art and beauty. The chorus would sing forth Beethoven's own lofty ideas, which he had asked a poet to formulate. For the melody, Beethoven looked back in time, to retrieve a theme from a previous composition—in fact, a love song. The notes of the Fantasy were barely dry during the dress rehearsal, with Beethoven himself improvising the piano introduction. (Actually, this first performance didn't go very well at all.)

We don't know how similar that improvisation was to the published version. What we do know, is that "keyboard improvisation was for him a central imaginative process."[27]

Beethoven left us a memoir about the structural idea of his improvisations: "Lied varied/at the end a fugue and/finishing pianissimo/each fantasy drafted in this fashion/and then carried through in the theatre."[27] Both the Choral Fantasy and the choral movement of the 9th Symphony begin with a simple lied, or song, which is developed through many variations. In the 9th Symphony, there are two double-fugues (in the battling orchestra variation, and when the Joy theme, and the second "Seid umschlungen" theme, are joined), although Beethoven does not compose a fugue in the Choral Fantasy. Another important element in improvisation was "imaginative freedom entailing abruptness, variety and surprise … well-thought-out deceptions, 'vernüftige Betrügereyen,' [which] had been identified by [J.S. Bach's son] C.P.E. Bach as belonging to a good fantasy."[28]

Listen to the end of the Choral Fantasy, from the point where the singers join in, as performed by the

---

27. Pascal. 108
28. Pascal, p. 109.

Schiller Institute's European chorus.[29] (See box of Choral Fantasy text)

Can you hear the Choral Fantasy with the 9th Symphony in your mind? Can you hear the similarities—simple, even similar themes, which undergo creative variations, uplifting ideas sung by soloists, and the full chorus, in contrapuntal interplay with instrumental soloists, and the full orchestra? Can you hear the Choral Fantasy not as an end product, but through the looking glass of the 9th Symphony, as embodying the potential for even greater future creative discovery?

We go back in time once more.

---

29. Start at 82:52 min.: http://larouchepac.com/node/18733.

Time node D: 1805: Fidelio

Read the following, from an article in *Fidelio* magazine:

Beethoven's only opera, Fidelio [first performed in 1805], is the story about how Leonora, a loving and brave wife, disguised as the young man Fidelio, saves her husband, Florestan, the political prisoner of a tyrant. The original play was based on the real-life story about how the American Revolution hero, the Marquis de Lafayette of France, was saved by his wife, Adrienne.

At the end, a chorus of prisoners and townspeople unite to sing "Wer ein holdes Weib errun-

---

Text of Choral Fantasy

Schmeichelnd hold und lieblich klingen
unseres Lebens Harmonien,
und dem Schönheitssinn entschwingen
Blumen sich, die ewig blühn.
Fried und Freude gleiten freundlich
wie der Wellen Wechselspiel.
Was sich drängte rauh und feindlich,
ordnet sich zu Hochgefühl.

Wenn der Töne Zauber walten
und des Wortes Weihe spricht,
muss sich Herrliches gestalten,
Nacht und Stürme werden Licht.
Äuss're Ruhe, inn're Wonne
herrschen für den Glücklichen.
Doch der Künste Frühlingssonne
lässt aus beiden Licht entstehn.

Großes, das ins Herz gedrungen,
blüht dann neu und schön empor.
Hat ein Geist sich aufgeschwungen,
hallt ihm stets ein Geisterchor.
Nehmt denn hin, ihr schönen Seelen,
froh die Gaben schöner Kunst
Wenn sich Lieb und Kraft vermählen,
lohnt den Menschen Göttergunst.

Flattering soft and sweet sound our lives' harmonies,
And ever-blooming flowers soar from our sense of beauty.
Peace and joy glide kindly like the waves' changing games;
What was rough and hostile, becomes a high feeling.

When the music's magic and word's blessing speak,
Something wonderful must happen, night and storm become light;
Outer quiet, inner bliss reign for the happy one,
The art's spring sun lets light rise from both (both music and words/poetry),

Great feelings, absorbed into the heart, will glow again new and beautiful,
Once a spirit has risen, it will always be echoed by a chorus of spirits.
So, happily accept, beautiful souls, the gifts of beautiful art.
When love and strength are joined, mankind has the God's blessing.

The dungeon scene from Beethoven's Fidelio.

gen, stimm in unserm Jubel ein" ("Who e'er a lovely wife has won, chime in with our jubilation!") The audience of the time would have recalled the nearly identical words of the second stanza of Schiller's ode, "Wer ein holdes Weib errungen, mische seinen Jubel ein!"

The musical theme comes from the last line of the most popular version of 'An die Freude,' The Ode to Joy, up until then. This chorus in Fidelio shows that Beethoven had 'An die Freude' stirring in his musical mind, which is highly appropriate, since the whole opera is a tribute to Schiller's ideals."[30]

As Schiller wrote, 'The path to political freedom is through beauty.'"

Go back in time again, stopping at age 24.

Time node C: 1794/95: Seufzer eines Ungeliebte und Gegenliebe

Beethoven composed an ironical song, uniting two related poems about unrequited love by Gottfried August Bürger. Listen to a recording with Dietrich Fischer-Dieskau singing, and to a performance by Feride Istogu Gillesberg and this author at an International Schiller Institute conference in Rüsselsheim, Germany, on July 3, 2011.[31]

Can you hear the third section of the song with the Choral Fantasy in your mind? In fact, probably knowing the Choral Fantasy first, you cannot help but have that in your mind, as you peer backwards in time to the song. Can you hear both with the 9th Symphony in your mind?

These ironical juxtapositions, referring backwards and forwards in time, change the past. We hear the compositions of the past with the compositions of the future in our mind, creating a delicious sense of musical development, not only within a single piece, but through revolutionary leaps from one musical idea to the next. A red thread of anti-entropic development of musical ideas and musical forms, and philosophical/poetical ideas, create a oneness out of the development of Beethoven's creative mind.

Was there an early Beethoven song based on Ode to Joy?

In 1803, Beethoven's friend, Ferdinand Ries, wrote to publisher Nikolaus Simrock in Bonn, offering eight lieder for publication which had been composed by Beethoven within the preceding four years. According one source, the set, published as op. 52, originally contained nine songs, one of which was a setting of Schiller's "Ode to Joy." The composer withdrew the Schiller

30. "An Early Setting of Schiller's 'Ode to Joy.'" *Fidelio* and "Beethoven's Celebration of the American Revolution." *Campaigner* August 1978, page 42.

31. http://www.youtube.com/watch?v=ozEm_snj9BM

A bust of Friedrich Schiller

setting before publication, and no manuscript exists.[32]

Go one year back in time, to age 23.

Time node B: 1793: The first evidence of Beethoven's yearning to set *An die Freude* to music.

On January 26, a man named Bartholomäus Ludwig Fischenich wrote to Schiller's wife Charlotte:

"I am enclosing with this a setting of the "Feuerfarbe" on which I would like your opinion. It is by a young man of this place [Bonn] whose musical talents are universally praised and whom the Elector has sent to Haydn in Vienna. He proposes also to compose Schiller's 'Freude' and indeed strophe by strophe. I expect something perfect for as far as I know him he is wholly devoted to the great and the sublime. Haydn has written here that he would put him at grand operas and soon be obliged to quit composing. Ordinarily he does not trouble himself with such trifles as the enclosed, which he wrote at the request of a lady."[33]

Note the Schillerian phrase "good and sublime" (das Große und Erhabene).

It would take Beethoven 31 more years to accomplish his mission.

Beethoven, who loved Schiller and Goethe more

than any other writers[34], once said, "Schiller's poems are very difficult to set to music. The composer must be able to lift himself far above the poet; who can do that in the case of Schiller? In this respect Goethe is much easier."[35]

Now just who was this Bartholomäus Ludwig Fischenich who sent the letter? The exciting thing is that Fischenich is a missing direct link between Beethoven and Friedrich Schiller! For his story, see Appendix I.

Five years later, Beethoven wrote two small sketches for the phrase, "Muss ein lieber Vater wohnen" from the Ode to Joy (from the 1798 Grasnick I sketchbook), which you can hear.

Time-node A: 1785: Friedrich Schiller writes *An die Freude*

In February of 1786, Schiller published the poem *An die Freude*, written the year before, in the second issue of his literary magazine *Thalia*.[36] This, of all of Schiller's works, though he criticized it himself, would become the most known throughout the ages, and throughout the world, precisely because a creative genius named Beethoven decided to crown his 9th Symphony with a section of the poem.[37]

Schiller, himself, wrote of the poetical idea behind *An die Freude*:

---

32. John Palmer on http://www.beethoven.ru/node/634

33. Thayer 120-121.

34. From a letter to his publisher requesting the complete works of both, which they did not send him. During his early career Beethoven acquired some volumes of Friedrich Schiller's collected works (including *Wilhelm Tell* and *Die Jungfrau von Orleans*), and later owned the entire series.

35. Beethoven to Czerny, 1809, in Thayer's *Life of Beethoven*, rev. and ed. by Elliot Forbes (Princeton, N.J.: Princeton University Press, 1967), vol. I, p. 472.

36. See the original publication of the poem in 1786.

37. In 1800, Schiller wrote to Körner calling the poem "detached from reality" and "of value maybe for us two, but not for the world, nor for the art of poetry," but, then he amended the poem in 1803, changing two of the lines in the beginning, and removing the last verse and chorus.

Let us be conscious of a higher ideal unity and by means of brotherhood we will attain to this state ... Joy is beautiful because it provides harmony, it is 'god-descended' because all harmony is derived from the Master of Worlds and flows back to him."[38]

Beginning with the immortal words "Freude, schöner Götterfunken," Schiller begins the poem by metaphorically speaking to Joy, the daughter of the gods, who appears as beautiful godly lightning (the which Prometheus stole in order to give knowledge to mankind, also a reference to Benjamin Franklin).[39] We become drunk with Joy's fire, as we enter her realm. It is Joy, or, the pursuit of happiness, as written in the American Declaration of Independence, which supplants the traditional class system, with brotherhood—uniting all humanity in the joy of republican freedom.

But Joy is also the motive force in the physical universe. It is Joy that causes the procession of the heavens. Joy smiles on the truth seeker from the truth's own fiery mirror. And Joy is entwined with love, or the Greek concept of *agape*[40]—beyond the heavens is a loving father.

Schiller had written the poem while visiting his very close friend and philosophical interlocutor, Christian Gottfried Körner (1756-1831). Actually, Körner was the first to compose a musical setting of the poem. In a letter to the publisher of *Thalia*, Georg Joachim Gishen, Schiller wrote, "The poem is beautifully set to music by Körner. What do you think about the idea of printing the music as well?"[41] which they did.[42] (See box)

It took Beethoven at least 31 years, but, with his increasing mastery of musical creativity, he would finally succeed in composing a masterpiece where Schiller's ideas and his music rose together to achieve a higher unity.

Schiller Speaks Directly to 'The Artists'

In 1789, four years after composing the "Ode to Joy," Schiller wrote the philosophical poem "The Artists," which develops the idea that it is through beauty, that one reaches truth. It both directs those seeking truth to immerse themselves in beautiful works of art, and speaks directly to the artist about his or her role in the process. This poem contains the seed-crystals of the ideas that Schiller would elaborate five years later in his seminal work, *The Aesthetical Education of Man*.[43]

Beethoven was 19 years old at the time, and although we don't know whether he read this particular poem then, or later, Schiller's ideas about the role of art, and the artist, would very likely have been discussed by Beethoven and his intellectual friends and mentors in his formative days in Bonn, and later in Vienna.

38. Quoted in Swafford, Jan, *Beethoven*, from Lockwood, *Beethoven: The Music and His Life*, p. 422.

39. Lyndon LaRouche wrote in Prometheus and Europe, "... contemporary European republican opinion modelled its references to Benjamin Franklin as a 'new Prometheus.' They spoke of Franklin in terms of 'God's sparks.' The latter reference is that adopted so famously by Friedrich Schiller in his 'An Die Freude,' and by Beethoven for his Ninth Symphony. This is also Schiller's pervasively implied conception of the Prometheus image itself."

40. Divine love, and love for your fellow man.

41. Baird, Olga, Early settings of the "Ode to Joy": Schiller-Beethoven-Tepper, *Musical Times*, Spring 2013.

42. Körner asked Schiller to write the poem for Körner's Masonic group, and Schiller dedicated the poem to Körner and his wife Dora Stock on the occasion of their wedding.

43. Translation and analysis by Marianna Wertz.

Körner's Ode to Joy

It was Körner's musical setting of the Ode to Joy which was sung to mourn Schiller in Humlebæk, Denmark, when the Danish poet Jens Baggesen and those gathered for a celebration of Schiller, received the shocking news that Schiller had died. They wrote a new text which read:[1]

Unser todte Freund soll leben!	Our departed friend shall live!
Alle Freunde stimmet ein!	All friends join in kind!
Und sein Geist soll uns unschweben	And his spirit shall surround us
Hier in Hellas Himmelhain.	Here in Hellas' heavenly shrine.
Tutissimi: Jede Hand emporgehoben!	Everybody raise his hand!
Schwört bei diesem freien Wein:	Swear by this free wine:
Seinem Geiste treu zu sein	To be faithful to his spirit
Bis zum Wiedersehn dort oben!	Until we meet again above!

As it turned out, they later learned that Schiller had not died, but was very sick, and could not rest because he needed to write in order to sustain his family. This, then, led Baggesen to organize the Danish Prince Friedrich Christian of Augustenborg, and Finance Minister Schimmelmann, to give Schiller a several-year stipend. As an expression of gratitude, Schiller wrote a series of philosophical letters to the prince, which laid the basis for his great work, *The Aesthetical Education of Man*.

---

1. "Danish Help to Schiller: How the Danish Marquis de Posa and Don Carlos Saved Friedrich Schiller," by Tom Gillesberg.

Before we end our discussion, it would be fitting for us to look at some of these ideas, because they help unveil the great purpose behind Beethoven's mission— in his image of God the Creator, to perfect his ability to use his creative powers, through the art of music, for the benefit of mankind.[44]

Only through Beauty's morning-gate
Can you penetrate the land of knowledge . . .
For what we here experience as beauty
We will one day meet again as truth.

At first, the light of truth is too blinding to look into directly, but beauty will pave the way. Through the joy of experiencing beauty, that which is experienced by the senses is ennobled, but in a playful way, which maintains the freedom of the individual.

The quality of beauty cannot be fixed, but must constantly be developed by the artist to reach higher and higher levels.

Yet higher still, to ever higher heights Creative genius soared.

From past creations one sees new creations arise,
Harmonies out of harmonies.

The artist's insight into his or her own power of creativity increases with each creation, enabling the next to be even more creative. It is not only the quality of the art which increases, but the quality of the creative thought process behind the art. There is an increase in what you could call, "creativity-flux-density."[45]

The wider thoughts and emotions open to the more exuberant interplay of harmonies, to beauty's more luxuriant stream— the more beautiful pieces of the universal plan . . . so lead him along the hidden course through every purer forms, pure music . . .

Beethoven understood this:

The true artist has no pride. He sees unfortunately that art has no limits; he has a vague awareness of how far he is from reaching his goal; and while others may perhaps be admiring him, he laments the fact that he has not yet

---

44. Thanks to Leni Rubinstein for the idea that Beethoven and Schiller are linked through the ideas expressed in "The Artists."

45. Analogous to LaRouche's concept of energy flux density.

reached the point whither his better genius only lights the way for him like a distant sun.[46]

Schiller wrote that if you elevate man with more and more beauty, "he will glide into the arms of truth." After arriving at reason, man sees that it was beauty that guided him there. Then, as Helga Zepp-LaRouche stated in her analysis of "The Artists," love, beauty, freedom and truth become the same. Schiller speaks directly to the artist:

> The dignity of mankind has been placed in your
>   hands;
> Protect it!
> It sinks with you! With you it will ascend!
> Poetry's sacred magic serves
> A wisely-laid universal plan;
> Steer it calmly towards the ocean
> Of the great harmony!

As Helga Zepp-LaRouche expressed it, "the task of art . . . : to improve and ennoble the human soul."

Beethoven was very conscious that this was his mission—that he would even have to "suffer the slings and arrows of outrageous fortune"—his deafness, and his other physical maladies, which caused him to shun social life—because he knew that he could not leave this world because of his art. Because his mission was not yet completed. He knew that he was not finished developing his art to the highest level that he was capable of. The goal of his art was nothing less than to improve and ennoble the souls of humanity.[47]

Beethoven's 9th Symphony, a gift from his creative spirit to the world, would do just that.

What would Schiller have said if he could have heard Beethoven's 9th Symphony? Well, we know that Schiller himself, one of greatest ever to wield the power of the word, understood that the power of music could lead us beyond the domain of words. Beethoven put it this way:

There is something mysterious in the effect of music, that it moves our inner self, so that it becomes a means of connection between two worlds. We feel ourselves enlarged, uplifted, rapt—what is that called other than in the domain of Nature, drawn to God? Music is a higher, finer language than words. In the moments, where every utterance of the uplifted soul seems too weak, where it despairs of conceiving more elegant words, there the musical art begins. From the outset, all song has this basis.[48]

This same idea is poetically expressed in Schiller's "Homage to the Arts," his last completed work, from 1804:

> The power of tones, which from the strings is
>   welling,
> Thou playest mightily, it well thou ken'st,
> What is the bosom with foreboding swelling,
> Is in my tones alone in full expressed;
> And if I start my scale of tones, I bear thee
> Upon it upward to the highest beauty.

Conclusion

Think of the long arc of the artist's development of an idea across an entire lifetime. Think about Beethoven's intention to set "An die Freude" to music. At each breakthrough, the artist reaches back and changes history—as in a fugue—where the theme is not the same by the time it reaches the end, even though it contains the same notes. So, also, the development of musical and poetical ideas throughout a lifetime of experimentation, and higher levels of the mastery of creative expression.

At each breakthrough, the precursors to that discovery change. We hear the echoes from the past, in the masterpieces of the future. And we hear the echoes from the future, in those earlier signposts along the way—the emanations of the creative spirit, yearning to break with the constrictions of "tradition," to experiment with bold, new ways to increase, as Shelley wrote, "the power of communicating and receiving intense and impassioned conceptions respecting man and nature," and to increase the power of human creativity itself.

—mich.ras@hotmail.com

---

46. Op cit. Solomon essay, footnote 24.

47. See Beethoven's Heiligenstadt Testament.

48. Letter to Caroline von Wolzogen, cited in Hellenbroich, Anno, "Beethoven's Creative Process of Composition: Reflections on Leonore (1806)and Fidelio (1814)"

Creating a New Unity For All Mankind

This discussion took place between Lyndon LaRouche and hundreds of political activists from across the United States, on the LaRouche PAC activists' conference call June 18, 2015. John Ascher was the host.

John Ascher: Good evening, this is John Ascher from Leesburg, Virginia welcoming everyone to this evening's fifth Fireside Chat with Lyndon LaRouche.

Lyndon LaRouche: We've now reached a point where the whole world is in a tremendous crisis. The United States is also in the tremendous crisis. Great changes are occurring all around. Some of them are not conclusive at the present point, but if you watch the patterns, you see that everything is going on in that direction.

For example: Obama is really in a very difficult situation. Certain kinds of developments, which are quite feasible to bring about, could ruin him. He's on the edge of being ruined. He's still the mad dog—not really a dog, perhaps a snake. Therefore that's factored in.

The point is, we're moving toward, the Democratic Party is moving against the Republicans who thought they had the total power over the whole thing at this time, and they don't have it. So, we have to approach things from that standpoint, not by playing like dogs and trying to steal other people's bones, but rather in the sense of thinking this thing through.

For example: One of the important things we should be doing, which we are not doing yet, even in fairly good circles in the Democratic Party—there are some good signs there on action, but it takes a little time to get that action moving—if we have the right actions, and begin to gnaw on the bones of Obama, or people like him—which is a dogged determination idea—then we probably can break out.

We're on the edge of the ability to pull a breakout. We're just short in terms of the Democratic Party, and people in our nation generally. We're very close to the point where we could, potentially, get Obama out of the picture. That is, weaken him to the point he does not have dictatorial claims anymore. That would make a big difference.

But there are other things that have to be done. We have to begin to deal with Wall Street. And Wall Street has to be tamed. And these are the things that *have* to happen, but they're not clearly pre-defined. But we understand them, and we know that these are the kinds of things, not necessarily all the things, but the kinds of things which will enable the people of the United States to get better control over the situation, and bring down Obama's funny games.

That would be the immediate intention. This would coincide with stopping Obama's tendency of bringing on global thermonuclear war. And right now, what you're talking about in the remainder of June, and July, is a period where Obama might still be able to provoke, together with the British, a general thermonuclear war. And a general thermonuclear war would be the extinction of the human species, or something very close to it.

So, that's where we are. These kinds of things have to be considered, and the problem we have with our people in the United States, is that most people in the United States have no willingness to understand what these factors are. They just wish something. They wish something is going to make it work. They hope that something will be done to make things better for them. They're getting pretty desperate about that already. They haven't had much experience with success, so far.

But there's something in the Democratic Party that has begun to move in a very serious way, and you're

LPAC/Chris Jadatz

Lyndon LaRouche at his November 2, 2012 press conference at the National Press Club, where he called for the removal of President Obama from office.

getting surprises—like a cat coming down on the back of some animal it's trying to eat—where the Democratic Party pounces on the Republican Party, and begins to eat it. So, it's a complicated process right now, but it's an understandable kind of process, which most of our citizens of course don't understand. But the knowable facts are already available for those who calmly look at reality: Maybe, maybe this is the kind of thing that will do the job, to get the United States out of the mess it's in now.

That's the kind of thing we have to think about.

Neither Animal Nor Machine

Q: Mr. LaRouche, D— from Oregon. My question is about artificial intelligence. Which assumptions, or axioms, that we currently believe to be true, would have to be overthrown in order to build machines that think creatively, that is, machines that employ the use of metaphor?

LaRouche: Well, actually, there are no machines designable which could actually do thinking. The human mind is completely different than any kind of these substances, these tricks, and absolutely different from any animal life. No animal life can simulate effectively human behavior.

For example, our pet dogs sometimes, if they are well-trained, will show things that look like human behavior, but it's not really human behavior. You identify the dog, a family dog, or hunting dog or something—

what you get is the dog responding to *human* behavior, but the dog will give an interpretation of human behavior which may not be actually human, but for the dog's purposes, he's responding; the dog is responding, to the human standards.

Actually the problem that gets in the way of people understanding reality—and I do mean reality—is that mankind is not an animal. That is, animals cannot create new ideas of principle. Only human beings.

For example: Take two cases of modern history. Take Kepler, Johannes Kepler. Kepler discovered the existence and the principles of the Solar System. We have made recently a development which is known as the Galactic System, the principle of the Galactic System, which is more powerful, a more influential power, for mankind than was simply Kepler's own discovery. So, what happens: Mankind, not some artificial system, is innovating conceptions which mankind had not recognized before, and using those conceptions in order to increase the productivity of mankind. And it is this thing that no animal can do. Animals can be trained, or influenced, to cause things that look like human behavior, but it's not.

So, let's take the case of Twentieth Century. Now, what happened is, the United States, for example, was, from the time of the beginning under people like [Alexander Hamilton], was increasing the power of mankind in the Solar System, on Earth. And this is what the Nineteenth Century amounted to. At the beginning of the Twentieth Century, what happened is that the United States plunged into a long, more than a century-long degeneration of the intellectual powers of the individual. There may have been technological advances in some respects, but the quality of the mind of the human being in the United States, for example, has been degenerating since the beginning of the Twentieth Century.

What we have to look at is the power of mankind, to understand the way that man himself can make discoveries which allow the human being to do something which no other human being has ever been able to do before. So the idea of mankind as [defined by] the mechanical, technological kind of thing, was wrong. And all the actual evidence shows that the idea of this popular opinion is just plain bunk.

'Music Is Life Itself'

Q: This is Lynn Yen. I'm the Executive Director of the Foundation for the Revival of Classical Culture, and we are presenting this upcoming Carnegie Hall concert on Father's Day, this Sunday, at 4 pm, and the theme is "Classical Music Against Violence." As a matter of fact, the theme of the concert is: Not War, but Music; Not Violence, but Music; Not Death, But Music—Because Music Is Life Itself. And the reason we're doing this concert is because today there has to be a way for people to become alive again. Non-violent music: There has to be something that doesn't bang, or crash, or shout, and not flashing, strobing lights; but actually where it's the human mind that is just an instrument, an idea that is the canvas upon which your imagination can paint a picture of life as it is.

Anyway, this concert of ours—which will include Bach, Brahms, Schumann, and Chopin—will be performed at the proper tuning of middle C at 256 cycles per second, which is going to be at A=430. We've had a lot of wonderful responses from schools. We have over 2,000 confirmations from the public schools, and a lot of these teachers, when we were talking to them about the concert, responded really ardently to the idea that something has to be done about violence, especially when we told them that we picked Father's Day, because men and young men, and fathers, are the major purveyors of violence.

They're the most at risk to suffer from violent death and violence. But they're also the most qualified to reverse it, in that a more dignified and less violent America needs to take place, replace the violent and thoughtless and completely out-of-control, insane one that we have in America today. And it has to be our menfolk who lead the charge.

So, whenever we discussed the idea of this concert with the teachers, they were really completely on board. As a matter of fact, this concert is also part of what we're going to be doing in going into the Summer, which is going to become a music and science program involving, we hope, a lot of young people from the New York City area. Now, Megan Beets and Jason Ross actually helped us and taught some of the classes last year in the music/science program, and we have students who really thrived. For example, José Vega, one of the students who just spoke at the Schiller conference in

creative commons/S.M.S.I., Inc.

IBM's "Deep Blue" computer was programmed in a doomed attempt to show its superiority over human intelligence in the chess game against Gary Kasparov in 2003, shown here.

November, and he articulately and beautifully developed the relationship between music and science and Kepler.

Now, the concert is being performed by Yaegy Park, Borislav Strulev, and Tian Jiang. Especially Yaegy Park, who is only 17, the violinist, I think has a really beautiful conception of music, and she talks about how she wants to perform the music, not for the money, not for being a professional musician, but because this is the thing that makes her want to be a human being.

I want to ask Mr. LaRouche the question, what is it that we really should be doing, going forward around this, and what were your general thoughts involved on what we're planning on doing going forward?

LaRouche: I think there are four examples—they're not adequate to span the entire subject matter, but I think these four cases will help to typify what the things are that we have to do in terms of the music, and the role of music.

First of all, Classical musical composition—just as a preliminary to this area of reply—there is a way of performing music which you may probably be familiar with, which was the Classical kind of music, which Megan Beets has laid out again, and that's very crucial.

On the other hand, people think that instruments produce music. Now they don't. The instruments are useful in helping mankind to capitalize on his potential. Now, you have areas, like you're talking about New York. New York City is, of course, one of the finest sources of organization of Classical musical composition. Unfortunately, over the course of the Twentieth

Violinist Yaegy Park performs at a Riverside Church concert in New York City, November 24, 2013. The concert was sponsored by the Foundation for the Revival of Classical Culture.

Century, Classical music was forced to degenerate. Only a few great musicians were actually capable of generating, freshly generating—some of my friends who unfortunately are deceased were among the best people of that type, and people like that. So, we have the Classical music from Italy, from Germany; there's some actual special cases. This is one category. They understand the principle which underlies the function of Classical musical composition.

Everything that is not Classical musical composition, in principle, is a fake. And what's happened in the Twentieth Century—real music has been *dying*, and not only dying in terms of behavior; it's been dying in terms of the human understanding of what this means, and the ability of the mental powers of the individual, to grasp. Most people who are musicians today, the popular musicians, do not have the ability to actually do creative things. They make noises. And they make exotic noises often—like most popular music.

Now you've got another thing. These great sources of Classical musical composition have been shrunken down to a very small part of the total population. In addition to that, we have something abroad, in China. Now China is not the United States, of course, but you will find a great development of Classical music in China. It's massive. Anciently China was one of the greatest resources of Classical culture, of Chinese Classical culture, and they spread it around. So that's a source.

Then, on the other hand, we must develop new capabilities for understanding what this whole thing's about. And you will find that the deep understanding of what the Classical principles were, or have been—I could name all kinds of great people—and when you can understand how they designed music in the relevant centuries, you can understand the idea of general conception of what we call Classical music, including in the Chinese variety. A very important part. Chinese musical development today has a great influence on the planet. This is one of the greatest sources of music, and it's come up in recent years in China.

So the idea is, our own organization is very deeply involved in developing, specifically for New York City and the environs, a fresh launching of real Classical music performance.

Now, not all of our people are fully professional, but a number of our people are professionals, and competent professionals, and they are connected to people who were the great people 40 years ago, 50 years ago. I could say more, but this is what you have to understand.

The final point I would make is: What is music? Now, some people think that it's a popular form of music—they rub instruments. But it's not that. What's there is the kind of thing that you got from the great Classical composition in Europe. And this spilled into the United States as well. New York City, and to some degree Boston, were the centers of Classical musical development in my span of life. So if we understand that, then what we should do is to understand that we have to revive the schools and development of Classical musical composition, understanding the actual principles—not the noise-making principles, but the actual principles of composition and performance which made the greatest Classical music before.

Now we may add something to the repertoire, as happened in history as such, which will change the characteristics of popularized form of Classical musical composition and performance. But that doesn't make much difference, really, with the principle of the thing. Because the point is this: Classical music is something that can only exist through the activity of the proper development of the individual human mind. And therefore, Classical music, composition, and the introduction of that to schools, to children in schools, as in New York, or in Boston, or, for a while, in Detroit. There was a very active Classical musical school in Detroit, which pretty much got shut down, when Detroit was pretty much shut down.

The point is, there is this principle that Classical music has nothing to do with barroom music, or

The Chinese Amber Quartet at the Asia-Pacific Chamber Music Competition in Melbourne, Australia, on July 14, 2013.

creative commons/Ryan Egan

making funny sounds, or that sort of thing. But, what we need is to revive the best of what we know, already from experience, in terms of Classical music composition in the past, in European development of Classical music, from Bach on, particularly, and going on to what we did in the United States in the best period—especially in the Nineteenth Century—and something we managed to keep alive, for a little bit, in the Twentieth Century.

What we have to do is realize that that approach to Classical music composition, as so defined, is a part of the moral development, and the mental development, of the average human person: To put this kind of thing into the periphery of the school system, from the beginning of school education, is *essential* for the *moral development of the powers of the human mind of the individual*. And that should be our mission.

And what you're talking about is one of those kinds of things that has been going on. Some people are trying to restore, and recover, Classical music composition in a competent way. And New York City is one of the areas where this is most possible. We ourselves are putting a lot of pressure now into—we have certain capabilities, but we don't have enough Classically trained performers, but we're trying to work on that thing, to increase the number of Classicaly trained and qualified performers, and this is something which should be in schools. It should be in all kinds of experiences in life, and get the junk, the noise, out of the minds of our people.

Lifting the Moral Powers of the Citizen

Q: Hello, Lyn, this is T— from California. It's a honor to speak with you.

My question is like this: We have been somewhat discouraged, I think lately, in trying to call Congress, because they just haven't been responsive, but now we see that the Democrats in Congress have significantly broken with Obama. We see that—and what I think we ought to be doing is to be calling Democrats in Congress *en masse* to tell them that the Party needs to take a new direction; that Obama has misled the party, and looking forward, we need to put in Glass-Steagall, and back a candidate who is going to put in Glass-Steagall—which is Martin O'Malley. This is the moment when we can call Congress, and hopefully turn the Democratic Party around. What do you think?

LaRouche: This is something which is technically feasible. It has growing potential to be realized, though I don't think it's very impressive what the potential is right now, so far.

But take into account the real nature of actually Classical musical performance and composition, which is far different than what most people in the United States understand today. What is understood as music today, among most people in the United States today, is essentially a form of noise; it's not music. Bum, bum, bum, bum, bum, bum—all these kinds of funny noises.

So, this is extremely important. It's important because this develops the moral powers of the citizen, or the student. And that's what you want—the moral powers correspond to actually a specifically, expressly Classical approach to human behavior. I just referred earlier to the question of what China had done historically, in terms of the approach to music, which is actually ancient. To our best knowledge, China is the most powerful ancient culture on the case. And we have the modern culture, and we have some things from an earlier period in music.

But this is a moral force, which makes people more

intelligent, or less un-intelligent today. It's important that this occurred. It's important that this development be understood, and be supported. Because when people understand what Classical music actually does, when performed properly, it produces an effect which otherwise is impossible to attain. And this effect has a *moral* force in society. And this moral force, which that kind of music represents, creates the moral impulses of the behavior of our citizens.

creative commons/Confederate till Death

KKK men and women at a cross burning on November 12, 2005.

The Upsurge of Racism

Ascher: We've got a couple of questions from our internet audience which refer to something that Lynn Yen, our musician from New York, referred to also. In her speaking about Classical music, she was referring to how part of their event on Sunday was to do something counter to all of the violence in society. So, we had a couple of people who wrote in asking about this horrible incident that occurred last night in Charleston, South Carolina, in an African-American church, and asking whether or not there is an effort in this country to divide people against each other, and if this is a deliberate effort to try to stir things up in terms of racism in the United States.

We got two questions on the same topic from people who are listening live right now, via YouTube. Would you like to say something about that?

LaRouche: I'm perfectly satisfied to say something about that.

Look, what's happening: This thing is both what it appears to be, but it's also what it may not appear to be. What's happened with that incident just reported: What that was, you have some stooge, some young person, a stooge, who sits in an African-American church, and then lurches up from within the audience, and starts killing people, including the pastor of the church. And people say, what's happening?

It's not that guy. That guy is an instrument, which is cultivated and used, and brought into the church. In other words, he was not really the author of the phenomenon. He was the instrument used by the people who created the incident.

Now, in the order of things in the United States, you have the history of slavery, legal slavery in the United States, where people from Africa were put into ships, put down in chains for transport across the Atlantic Ocean, down into some parts of the United States. Most of this was done by the British, the British agencies. So, this is the history.

Now, therefore, because of the Southern states of the United States, from Virginia on down, Virginia on down, all the way down, has been historically, up to the present day, a concentration center for racism. Now, what's the function of racism? Now, for one part, people say, it's for slavery. That's too simple. Yes, slavery is a big factor, but that's not what the point is.

Remember, once the Revolution under Lincoln occurred, the so-called Negro slaves began to become not only freed, but also geniuses, because there were leaders among the former slaves, or the slave centers, who would actually develop a fierce desire to get *out* of what the evil was that they were being subjected to—as opposed to being slaves as such. And even those who had been slaves as such, began to rise. Because when people went from slavery to freedom—that is, true freedom, not some kind of Southern dirty trick—under those conditions, you would find the mental powers of the Negroes in the United States increased, and they increased at an accelerated rate.

All right. Now this is part of it.

UNHCR/A. D'Amato

The lucky ones: 186 people rescued by the Italian Navy during their attempt to cross the Mediterranean to Europe.

Now, you look at the whole history. Look at this context that I just described, in terms of the history of the trans-Atlantic region, and beyond. What happened? What happened was —look what you're seeing right now in the area of Europe, and you have massive shipments of people from Africa, being shipped into Italy and other places, and then being thrown *back* from these other places, such as France, and condemned to death. And the rate of death rates by these transports across the Mediterranean has meant a rise of mass murder.

Now what you're getting is: you put the two things together. We're seeing that inside the United States, you're also getting a mass murder phenomenon of this type. And this guy, whoever he was, this young guy, who sat in the black church, and then rose to kill off the pastor and kill other members of the body—he was not cause of this thing. He was the instrument of this thing. He was the animal, who operated under "orders" from a higher sense.

So if you look at the whole process, inside the United States, you see there is a massive increase of this kind of horror show coming out. And it comes especially in the border areas, including Texas—and Texas is a borderline case.

Therefore, the problem is that there's an international, largely British-directed, British-steered [operation], into the United States, in particular, as well as in the Mediterranean cases, which is across the Mediterranean Sea. And this is global.

This includes California where we have a governor who is organizing mass killing of citizens in that state, by trying to deprive them of water. And even though there are excuses for this thing, there *are* no excuses for it. There is no problem of water. Even the Pope is being sucked into this. He has a Nazi who's giving the instructions to the Pope on how to deal with this thing. But the Pope is intimidated. So he is capitulating to terror, in fact. And we should free him from that sort of thing. I had some close friends in the papacy who at one point, including the Pope, we were working with, and it was far different then than what's going on now.

The point is, we have to realize that there are forces, typified by the British Empire, which in legendary periods of time, and also earlier, which have done this kind of method of mass assassinations of human beings, reducing populations. That is going on now! That is going on under the governor of California, for example, who is doing exactly that.

So what was happening in that church, that we just referred, was a foolish little boy, who rose from the pew, and committed mass murder. Actually conducted it. Killed the pastor and so forth. This is now a horror show. But the horror show is being used to promote a replication of that kind of horror show, to spread it more broadly.

And therefore, we have an enemy within, within the United States as well as other places. And you don't sit back and say, we're impotent; there's nothing we can do about this; this happened, this happened, this happened. This guy did it, but this guy may have done the action—but he wasn't the cause of the action. When you look at the territory, you say, oh, this is typical Southerner behavior. It's not that, but that's the way it works. You have the race hate, the hatred factor, in the Southern states, especially as you don't have it in the northern states.

Texas, for example. Racism in the lower states. Racism, racism, racism. Florida, racism—the rate of murder is highest in Florida, and it's not on the beaches of Florida. It's among the bitches of Florida.

So, these are the kinds of things we have to take into account.

Obama Ready To Be Dumped

Q: Hi, this is A— in southwest Minnesota, and I'd like to ask a question about this business of free trade, that's plagued us now for 15 years with NAFTA in North America, and I viewed that as a looting of the American people, the American companies. And now we're talking about trans-Pacific free trade. And I can't quite get my arms around the idea of how the trans-Atlantic would probably be running this, and the United States would pass a law that could loot countries all over the world. And I just can't see how they can pull this off, especially with the BRICS countries. So, I just wanted to know if you could comment on this?

LaRouche: Yeah, sure. I think a lot of the problem currently today is from Obama, himself. It's Obama *and* his intimate allies, the Republican Party. Now, that doesn't mean the Republicans as such are categorically of this nature, but there's a certain group—well, I won't name the actual name of the section of the party, but there are people in the Republican Party, in the Congress, who have no business being even in the United States! They are trash; they are blue trash, white trash, pink trash, all kinds of things, but they're Republicans.

And you see the picture now. Here you have Obama. Obama is supposed to be a Democrat! He's not a Democrat, he's a Republican, right? So, what's going on?

Now, the real Democrats don't like any of this stuff. They're not in favor of Republicans. But they don't blame the Republicans as such. They blame the caste system, which controls, top down, the Congress of the United States.

And what the issue is now is that Obama is a racist: He's against human beings, essentially. Not against black, or white, or pink or anything: He's against human beings. And look, if you know the truth about it: I knew the truth about him, from the first time I encountered him when he was first put into power in the United States. And I had an attack on him, because I exposed the fact that he was promoting death rates.

That was what his policy was and I attacked that, and he really got very angry about that and tried to kill me and tried to poison me and all these kinds of things happened; that's what he did. I got out of that. I knew what would happen to me in the attempt to poison me in that way, didn't really work, because I sort of recovered rather quickly; I had a year of real problems as a result

White House/Pete Souza

Obama confers with his buddy House Speaker John Boehner after participating in a session with the House Republican Conference on March 13, 2013.

of what the poisoning was. But that was all over.

But I was out there, and I was the first threat against Obama once he was elected. And so he backed into a rage, because there were some very influential circles at that time, in the Administration, and they were attacking the health-care policies of Obama; and the health-care policies of Obama right then, were already genocidal: That is, for mass genocide trends. And he's always been of that nature, ever since he became President.

Now, what's happened now, is, he's now being dumped. He's being thrown out the window. But he's in the last phase of a desperate effort to cause global thermonuclear war. In other words, the danger from Obama now, is, as long as he remains President of the United States, or with Presidential powers, he is committed,—absolutely profoundly, energetically committed, to launching international thermonuclear war, between the period of now into probably, say, July, maybe as late as early August; where the people of the United States right now, are in danger of being exterminated, or virtually exterminated, by a thermonuclear war, which is organized chiefly by the British Empire, and you remember, Obama is a British Empire stooge. He always was; he was shipped in.

His mother was married to a terrorist in Asia, and his

tradition has always been that; he's a terrorist intrinsically. He's a human hater, a hater of human beings. His father was part of that same stuff. So what do you expect?

So the problem now is that Obama is no longer a Democrat. As of the recent period, he is no longer a Democrat! He's a Republican? Well, how did a Republican President get to be in that transition?

So we have to get rid of Obama. And that is on the edge. There are notable Republicans, in particular, who are ready to dump Obama at the first opportunity, and that's the thing that has to occur. *If* we dump Obama, and the point is that Obama is essentially a Republican; he has no connection, really, to the Democratic Party any more. And this is the problem that's going on there: How can the Republican Party respond to the fact that Obama is a Republican, and there are very few Democrats among the Democratic Party?

So that's the situation. What we need to understand, is that we have to arouse our own citizens, who are not necessarily Republicans by any means, and certainly *not* Obama-ites, get them out of power, get them thrown out of power. And we in the United States, I know, with what the movement is inside the Democratic Party now, and some other locations, are ready to move and dump Obama, and to dump the kind of Republicans that breed with Obama. And that's our best shot.

Q: This is V— from New York City. I'm very interested in knowing your opinion of the special interest groups.

LaRouche: Well, that's a broad term, and I think it tends to get confusing. But there are ways of looking at something we might call the so-called interest groups of that type, but I don't think it's truly categorical. I think probably, your experience might suggest that it's categorical. And there are people who adopt a policy of belief that is not their own, but it's like the guy that goes out and gets a special kind of suit that he runs around in, and he calls himself something like that. But it's all foolishness on that side.

So I mean, we're in a situation where, if we can get our citizens to move a little faster in insight—and there are movements such as part of our economic system which do understand what has to happen. And these people are willing to move and are capable of moving. But we have to get some of the weight off their backs. There are many Americans now who realize, that the condition of life of the typical citizen of the United States, has been in a long wave of degeneration, of the standard of living of the American citizen, which began in the beginning of the Twentieth Century and has become ever worse, ever since up to the present time.

So the time has come for the American citizen to revolt against this kind of suppression, against the economic policies which were introduced during the Twentieth Century; because we've been in a consistent decline and deterioration, of the conditions of life of the average citizen of the United States, and it's been getting worse all along the way. And many of you have lived for any period of say, 20 years, 30 years, 40 years, 50 years, you can trace that very readily: Conditions of life for the typical American have become progressively worse, as Wall Street has enriched itself by gambling.

Wall Street's Bankrupt, Not Greece

Q: Hello, this is J— from New York City. And I've received information about Greece having declared that their debt owed to the International Monetary Fund is "illegal, illegitimate, and odious." And obviously, they didn't use Glass-Steagall, but it seems to run along the lines of what you have been talking about in regards to how the banking system is run. What's your take on that?

LaRouche: The first thing that must be done, is we have to shut down Wall Street. Because what's happening? Wall Street is not producing anything. That is, in net effect, they're producing nothing; as a matter of fact, they're detracting. Wall Street is destroying the economy of the United States. And what we should do and must do, and what the Presidency must do once Obama's kicked out, is get Wall Street shut down.

Because look at what Wall Street does. They don't do anything for the U.S. economy. Nothing! Much less than nothing! So the thing is, we should be shutting down Wall Street.

Now, Glass-Steagall as a law, Franklin Roosevelt's law, would eliminate that problem. So what we want to do, is don't buy these guys out—bankrupt them! Shut them down. The minute we shut them down, you will find out what has happened, is that the people of the United States are being looted, by means of use of Wall Street money, Wall Street investment. So, shut down Wall Street, get it out of business: bankrupt it, shut it down, and change the character of the economy. To what? To technological progress in labor and skills.

We've been going in the other direction. Just think, if you look back at your own history, what has been the

EIRNS/Suzanne Klebe

LaRouche PAC's January 20, 2015 rally at Federal Hall, New York City, right across from the New York Stock Exchange.

trend in terms of the relative productivity of labor, per capita, in the United States, during your lifetime so far? You have been going through an increasing rate of destruction of your standard of living and your circumstances, and moral circumstances of life in the United States. What's the key point? The key instrument is Wall Street! Now Wall Street should be cancelled. And Glass-Steagall *would do that*.

So you want to get Glass-Steagall into operation right now, as an anti-Republican operation. And then, you will get an opening, under which we will have the financial mobilization required to increase the productive powers of labor in the United States. And the increase of the productive powers of labor in the United States, is the increase of the standard of living, of the people of the United States: Better education, better life, better health care, all these kinds of things. And these are things which are already available to man in terms of technology in the United States.

But we have to get Wall Street shut down. Glass-Steagall, if properly enforced, will do that. It will also bankrupt most rich Republicans. That won't hurt anybody! That will be useful. The Republicans who get bankrupted, they'll have to change their careers and they'll be more moral, as opposed to the less moral trend that they have been showing recently.

Q: This is W— from Virginia. Mr. LaRouche, I have another question concerning the Greek crisis. We know that this dynamic of the crash of the trans-Atlantic system is what's driving all this push for war. But recently the Tsipras government made a comment that the IMF is a criminal organization, and I think that signals that they're fed up with these talks. And they have a meeting with the Russians, but at that point, the Greeks could potentially join the BRICS. I'm just wondering, what effect that will have on the Merkel government and the threat of war, if it hasn't already happened by then.

LaRouche: [laughs] Yeah, you hit the key note with that supplementary remark!

Well, what's happening is this. Now, Greece has been a slave economy, for some time. It was induced by corrupt elements inside the Greek population, but that was only an incidental feature. What you're dealing with is a threat of a mass murder of the Greek population.

Now, this comes under a British category, the British Empire, and Wall Street, of course is a product of the British Empire. And Wall Street is the means of destruction of the means of life and so forth, and education, of people in general. And you have to understand what the British Empire is. Actually, the United States has been living under the influence of the British Empire, imperial control, over a very long period of time. At one point, of course, in our history, we fought and defeated the British forces. But lately, we've done a very poor job of dealing with that kind of problem.

So that's where the problem arises in that sort of thing. So if we don't deal with this problem, we're going to get mass death. Right now, the solution for the Greek condition, in terms of very narrow and specific circumstances, the Greeks themselves, the leading Greeks are saying "to hell with their persecutors." And the chief hell-raiser is the British Monarchy, Her Majesty. And the racist, mass killer, in the trans-Atlantic region, is the British Royal Family.

June 26, 2015   **EIR**   "We Are All Greeks"   61

German Chancellor Angela Merkel with her partner British Prime Minister David Cameron, at 10 Downing Street.

creative commons/Crown copyright

This is not anything unique for people who know what the story is: The British Royal Family, that is the presently living members of the British Royal Family, have a policy of degeneration, and mass murder of the populations of the planet: That's their policy. It *has been* their policy, it's their *declared* policy, it's their publicly declared policy. And that's what the problem is.

Now, at the same time, the use of speculation, wasteful speculation, becomes the mechanism by which the economy of Europe is being ruined: Portugal, ruined; Spain, ruined; France, very deeply injured; Italy, great injury, and so forth and so on. And so what you have is Germany, which still has some strength. I'm not saying that Germany is the great ideal of modern European culture, but it happens to be that in Europe, this side of Russia, the only nation which really has a significant growth pattern in it—and that's not too good right now.

But there are certain people—not Merkel; Merkel is not a very good thing to have in Germany, for Germans. Shmerkel or Merkel, whatever you want to call her. So that's where the problem is, that's how the Greek problem comes into play.

So Greece was looted, and raped. It was raped because pressures from Britain, in chief, had induced certain parts of the Greek population to assassinate their own fellow Greeks, but by economic means.

So the means has been the British system, chiefly, but also most of the nations of Europe west of Russia, have committed a crime of mass murder against Greeks, by starving them to death, and similar kinds of things.

Now, the Greek population and the new present government, says: No, we're not going to do that; we're not going to tolerate that, we're not going to accept it. We're going to resist it. And then, the nations of Western Europe, in chief, especially Britain, and anything related to them, all these things— you can get the list of these criminals, easily. So what you have is the demand that the Greeks submit to British mass murder of Greeks!

Now some people don't like that, and the main support for the Greeks, comes from Russia. Because the power of Russia, even though it's not intending to start a war against Western Europe or something, is in a sense, a fact. And you have the same thing in a lot of the whole area of Europe, and Eurasia: Russia through much of Eurasia, China, India, many parts of South America now are also on the march to progress and success.

So the issue right now, is if we were reasonable, we would immediately *wipe out* the debt attributed to the Greeks. Because there is no honest reason why that money should be collected. The problem is, you have people in Germany who understand that that's wrong, but they don't have the guts, so far, to do anything about it. And Merkel is not exactly helping anything good. She would be better out of German politics than in it. And we could have other people in Germany, who may not be the greatest people in the world, but these are patriotic Germans, and therefore they would prefer to defend the interests of Germany and adjoining nations, because Germany's characteristic is, still now, its industrial characteristic. So the industrial characteristic of Germany is unique, in terms of that part of the world. So if you unleash the potential of the German economy for this kind of production, then you are going to help *all* nations of Europe, by doing so.

You will then eliminate the danger of a *worldwide thermonuclear war*. Because if Russia and Germany, and other nations like China and so forth, come into play, the war is not going to happen. And all you have to do is throw Obama out, down the trash can, and then, everything goes much better. It may not be perfect, but it'll be much, much better, and for the coming generations of mankind.

And that's what the situation is: We're on the edge, where the Greek issue is a very important signal of what the problem is that all mankind on the planet faces. The Greeks are doing *very* well; the Greek government, is doing very well, and has friends, and it's moving in directions which are very difficult conditions for it to deal with. But they have a movement, a spirit and a determination, and many nations, like Russia, other nations in Eurasia, are very much involved in realizing what the Greeks are.

kremlin.ru

Siemens CEO Joe Kaeser (center, back to camera) meets with Russian President Vladimir Putin (third from left) and colleague in March 2014.

You remember, the Greeks have played [a major role] for a very, very long time, in Europe and beyond. And the Greeks have been the master of civilization for most periods of life. The Greek legacy, despite the deterioration of the quality of life in Greece—how did Europe get a modern civilization? It came through the Greeks.

Now, the Greeks at that time were not exactly in the best condition, but some people, like Nicholas of Cusa went into the Greek area, where the culture of the Classical Greek was still being maintained. And Nicholas of Cusa created modern Christianity, and since that time we've had improvements in European civilization, and in the United States. So: That's the story.

And the problem of everything that those Europeans who are attacking the Greeks are talking about—they're a criminal proclivity! That's what the problem is!

The Murder Policy

Q: Hi, Mr. LaRouche. This is E— in the Bronx, New York City. I would like to ask you, what do you think about all this gang violence, that's going on throughout the country. Many innocent people are getting shot by handguns, and a lot of people have died. I believe that Congress should pass a law, doing away with guns for the American public—they have no need of them—and it should be signed into law by the President. In other words, guns shouldn't be made anymore, they shouldn't be manufactured any longer. And all those storeowners, that acquired their weapons legally, to ward off crimes, they would simply be required to turn them in to the government, and the government would do away with them. It should be a crime to have a gun. I believe they

should be done away with completely. So, I would like to know what is your take about that?

LaRouche: I don't think that is the problem. I think the misuse of guns is a very significant problem—the misuse. And, there, of course, are orders between one thing and the other, where the use of guns and access to guns, has to be under some degree of control, of social control, which is a matter of the security of the body of the citizenry.

But there are also weapons which are equally dangerous to guns. So the limitation on guns will not remove the problem. Because there are other means—just, for example, poison. Poison is much more efficient than guns for mass killing of people in the United States, and elsewhere. The gun is symbolic, in its use; it's symbolic of what the problem is. But the gun, per se, is not the problem. The problem is, how the gun is used. But how the gun is used is a very small part of the problem of murder, mass murder.

Health care! Lack of health care, is murderous. Lack of support to fight against infectious diseases, is murderous. The lack of health care, the destruction of the quality of health care in the United States, is crucial. Because the ability of the citizen to get health care, is shrinking all the time, at an accelerating rate right now. And Obama has been one of the promoters of that mass killing of citizens in the United States, who are helpless, and deprived of access to things they need, in order to stay alive. The improvement generally of medical care, of health care; you know, dangerous problems that mankind has. The improvement of health care, in terms of scientific means.

And often, our government, itself, through secret or-

U.S. Navy/Steve Johnson

Policies that kill: The homeless of Salinas, California line up for food from a U.S. Navy program in 2009.

people? Withdraw health care. You want to increase the death rate? Deal with health care. Eliminate the protection. Fail to give people the help they need, to deal with dangerous illnesses, these kinds of things. And the spread of disease, in that form. The spread of disease is probably one of the most efficient methods of mass killing—and *in* the United States, and *by* the United States.

No. What you are talking about is a legitimate concern, but don't make it simplistic. Guns are not the sum total of willful mass killing, or just ordinary killing. Other means are much more efficient.

ganizations, secret bureaus, run under the federal government, and similar institutions, is also a big killer. And, you don't have to use a gun to kill people by that method. Use poison, use deprivation, use spread of disease. And the spread of disease, willfully, is one of the best ways of killing people in the United States, *en masse*. And that is going on!

The quality of health care available to the people of the United States, has *collapsed* during the recent time, especially since the Obama Administration, and even before that. So the deliberate mass murder of citizens, by misuse of what is called health care, *is the greatest single threat to human life* inside the United States, today.

The gun is not the issue. The misuse of it is a significant problem. But the real problem is the use of instruments, by our government itself, as under Obama. Obama is killing people—he doesn't use a gun, he uses himself. And he is the weapon that does the mass killing.

So, it's true, we don't want uncontrolled gun use, but the assumption that gun use is the problem, is a mistake. It's relatively minor. Unless you go into general warfare, the gun is not really a significant thing in history. But what is significant, is the various means by which governments and other agencies *do mass killing*. And they don't nicely go out there and just shoot you on the street. That's not the way it happens. That does happen, but that's not the way it happens.

And you have to regulate the question of health care: Do people get health care? You want to kill

Q: Yes. Mr. LaRouche. It's a pleasure, again, to get to ask a question of you, and thanks for these fireside chats, they're awesome, really great; thank you. The question I have—you briefly discussed it a little bit ago, about Pope Francis, and his position—I guess he's taken the environmentalist position, that there is man-made climate change? Could you expand a little bit more, on what you were talking about earlier?

LaRouche: I don't understand wholly, exactly what the Pope's position is. I understand there are a group of forces, which pushed the Pope to—I don't know how far his agreement goes—but I know he's being pushed into doing that.

Now, you have a guy called Schellnhuber, and Schellnhuber is a British agent, in profession. He's also a mass killer. His design is mass killing.

And the policy here—the fraudulent policy—I don't know how the Papacy, in somehow or some way, or some degree, actually bought into this idea, but the very idea that's in the public press; I don't know what the Pope thinks, I don't know what the circles of the Pope actually think. I know that the Pope is under tremendous pressure because of economic policy questions, where Italy and other parts of the world are under great pressure, because of conditions like the British conditions impose.

But, I will not say what the Pope's intention is, what his motive is. I know what the pressure is that's on him, from Schellnhuber, who's a British agent, and a mass killer. And I don't think the Pope is a mass killer. But I know Schellnhuber *is*, and that's the problem.

Get Rid of the Queen!

Q: I'm from West Palm Beach, Florida. I have a question about the economic cycle, I'm not sure if you're familiar with "Shemitah"? Trying to find anything about, the Jewish calendar of economic cycles, that pertain to seven-year cycles? The Jewish calendar, are you familiar with the Shemitah?

LaRouche: There's a lot of mythical stuff to that stuff. It doesn't work that way. What did happen, was well-known—it was Adolf Hitler who demonstrated that one. It was Adolf Hitler's policy. You have a Hitlerian policy. And Jewry today, of course, is international. That is, there's no such a thing as a "universal"—there's a Jewish religious belief, and that's a religious belief. But the great horror was, of course, that now, everything today comes as a reflection of the *mass murder* of Jews by Hitler! And by the British! That's a big factor.

And also what happened is the part played in terms of the Jewish settlement, the increased settlement in terms of that part of the population there, in present Israeli life; again, the same kind of thing. And you have Jewish policies which come from manipulation of certain sorts, and then on the other hand, if I look at certain Jewish communities, they are developing and making a very significant contribution to the improvement of water supplies in arid areas! You have some people in Australia doing the same thing. You have people in Mexico who have proved themselves to be experts in this business!

So, the promotion of human life, and the Jewish society, are very closely related. You can't make a Jewish distinction. Sure, you have people who are mass murderers; you have people who are enraged, Jews who are enraged—who were enraged by the Hitler massacres. And they became angry.

I dealt with very important Jewish leaders in the immediate post-war period. I was a close friend of these groups of the Jewish leaders, military leaders and so forth, in that period. And that was the one period, the so-called "socialist period." Then you got the new thing that came in, the hardball nuts, and they screwed everything up for Israel, and they imposed upon Israel, a mode of

creative commons/Janwikifoto
Depopulation advocate John Schellnhuber, CBE, at the Nobel Laureate Global Symposium in Stockholm in May 2011.

life which is contrary to what the Israelis of the founding of Israel, the modern founding of Israel, were going to do!

Remember, you had all these Jews who had been *murdered, mass murdered*; mass murdered on a degree which is *unbelievable*, actually, to any human being in a normal case. Now these guys, who are people I worked with and associated with, in the immediate post-war period, and they were my friends, I know what they were like, the so-called Socialist Jewish organization. These guys were warriors, but they weren't killers. They were defending—they're saying, "Look, all these Jews were killed by Hitler, and by his friends, including Saudi friends." And, they were trying to live.

What happened was things went bad when the so-called Socialist group in Israel was pushed aside for this right-wing wild-man crowd. And they are a problem; they are a pestilence. And if you know the history of Jewry, in Palestine, you have some great heroes in that process, even under conditions which were not good. You have great humanists among Jews in that area.

This idea of racial or similar kinds of things, is absolutely nonsense. Yes, the Saudis are stinkers, the Saudis are mass killers. If you want to worry about something, the Saudis are the mass killers! But they're not really so bad, because the Saudis are nothing but agents for the British Empire, of Her Majesty the Queen. Now, if you want to get rid of the problem, get rid of the Queen!

Focus on the Historical Characteristic

Q: Hello! This is T— from New Hampshire. I'm truck-driving in New Jersey right now, and my pitbull is in my lap, in a traffic jam right now. Mr. LaRouche, it's an honor to speak with you. I just wanted to comment on the gun thing. Why is it, that in society, when we have—well, first of all, if you look at the gun statistics, of the late, they are down in the last 10-20 years. Number one.

Number two is, why is it that when we have a mishap, such as of late, we want to get rid of the thing? And it's not just with guns, it's with pitbulls; we'll use that as an example, because we have mishaps all over

President George H.W. Bush, son of Nazi financier Prescott Bush, and Barbara Bush host a state dinner for Queen Elizabeth and Prince Philip on May, 14, 1991.

George Bush Library/College Station, Texas

the country with pitbulls, and now it's at the point where media, the government, everybody is saying, "Oh, they're a bad breed, you have to get rid of them, they're no good.'" It's not the breed, it's the people who aren't in control of such! And I'll take my comment off the air.

LaRouche: Let me give you a whole biographical slant on what you're talking about. During the 1970s, I ran for President of the United States, and that Presidential campaign made quite a stir at that point.

In the following period shortly after that, I was approached by some people who were historically leaders of the Presidency, in intelligence sector, during the period of World War II. These people, as senior people who were part of Franklin Roosevelt's close followers, came to me in 1977; and they came to me and asked me, would I work to do certain things for the United States, in terms of a new administration in the United States, which was the Reagan Administration. And, as most people know, Reagan was soon shot, with an intent to kill him, actually. And he was very much weakened in his ability to maintain much of his functions from that point on. And what happened is that Bush came in, as in an infestation, which entered into the Presidency.

Now, this was a very bad thing. The original Bush of the Bush family's dynasty, or genocide if you want to call it that, was allowed to bring in a member of the Bush family to the Presidency; that is a child of the Prescott Bush Nazi-type, who was operating from Britain.

So, what happened is that the President, under those conditions, the President of the United States, Ronald Reagan, at that time, was shot by a representative of the family of Bush! And so, he was crippled for a while, and the whole system that we were operating on was then frustrated, because the Bush factor entered into the Reagan administration through the assistance of the attempted assassination of Ronald Reagan, at that time.

As a result of that process, I had been running as a specialist on science programs, international science programs, then. And I was working with one of the leading scientists of the world at that time. And we, in part, were sharing assignments which we had organized, together with Ronald Reagan, to negotiate an agreement with the remains of the Soviet Union, to avoid war between the United States and the Soviet Union at that time. And that was good, it was good.

But what happened is the Bush interests moved in through the aid of the British, and what they did is that they put in a new head of the Soviet Union, as an emergency thing, from Britain. And the British influence on that leader, just stuck in there, changed the entire policy, from the Reagan administration policy, which I had been an active part of, together with a leading scientist of the world, who was shall we say, my co-worker. And that's how things happened.

So, when you want to understand these kinds of things, you have to understand the movement of the Bush family, which is actually a *Nazi-like family*: The Prescott Bush family, he was *literally a Nazi*, at that time. And the Bush family has the stink of the Nazi characteristic ever since that time to the present day, including the current Bushes. And I don't believe in burning the Bushes, because I don't want the stink up there. But that's the situation.

So, if we look at world history, as you might look from a practical standpoint from your profession, your activity, that's what the problem is. We had two good Presidents after that. And they were both people I worked with, and that's the history. The problem is, we have not had decent Presidents, except for two cases of installation, since the time that Reagan was shot.

That may be interesting for you; I think perhaps your practical circumstances in life might make that interesting for you.

The Common Purpose of Mankind

Ascher: Lyn, besides what you've been discussing a lot with your associates and organizers about the music project in New York, the other major statement

NASA

The common aims of mankind: The joint U.S.-USSR Apollo-Soyuz Test Project docking mission on July 17-18, 1975.

that you have put out in the last days is entitled, "Dump London's Phony Debts with Glass-Steagall; The Euro Is Bankrupt, Not the Drachma." And in that statement you said: "The critical action is Glass-Steagall in the United States, and force it in European countries"; and of course, that's in reference to the Greek crisis, which you referred to already earlier in our discussion. I wanted to reference that for everyone on the call, that they can get further information on the website.

So, Lyn, we've covered tremendous amount of ground here this evening. Do you want to say anything here in conclusion?

LaRouche: I just want to add a closing note which might be useful on the overall perspective we've covered this evening. So far, we've covered a number of subjects, and I want to emphasize that all of these subjects are related, including the questions made by the people who were the questioners: that all of this material is relevant. It's part of life. There may be some missing elements in the record we presented this evening, but the same principle exists under even different conditions. We as a nation must pull ourselves together to face the questions which we should be considering in life, even the questions we hadn't even known about beforehand, which is frequently the case.

And we should get mankind to unify himself, not about the individual as the individual, but to bring the people of the United States in particular, together. Even though they have different backgrounds, different kinds of considerations, they are the same people and *should be* the same people. They shouldn't be different groups of people: They should be people of the United States, and the families of the United States, and the culture of the United States, and the people of the United States. That's what it has to be.

The idea of the "rugged individual" is a stinking idea. The role of the individual, who can express a participation in the love for all mankind, which is expressed by promoting people to become educated, to understand what the principles of mankind should be, under the conditions of the contemporary era. That is the issue.

And all of the things we discussed tonight in particular, are into that one thing: Don't try to assume that everybody is different. They're all different in some way, but their needs are similar; their future, the possibility of their future is the same. The condition of the world as a whole, not only in the United States, is the same.

What we have to do is build up nations of the planet, like our United States, like the states of South America, like Australia, like the Middle East, like China, like India, like Russia, and so forth, and Europe: All these things are things which have to come together, because in the final analysis, we live not only on Earth, but mankind lives in the Galaxy also, and we're now beginning to understand what the Galaxy means: that mankind lives under the domain of the Galaxy, as it lived, also, under Kepler's understanding of the way the Solar System was created and functioned.

So it's all one thing, with many differences in shading and characteristic, but the object is to *bring mankind as a species, into a growing, developing process*, for the future of mankind and for the future of what mankind can accomplish in the Galaxy, and other locations of relevance.

And so we should have this kind of unification, of concern, not particularization, but the search to come together from different standpoints, from different skills, but all coming to a common purpose at the same time.